W9-AGZ-647

HOW TO WRITE ARTICLES THAT SELL

HOW TO WRITE ARTICLES THAT SELL

Second Edition

BY
L. PERRY WILBUR
& JON SAMSEL

ALLWORTH PRESS
NEW YORK

© 1999 L. Perry Wilbur and Jon Samsel

All rights reserved. Copyright under Berne Copyright Convention, Universal Copyright Convention, and Pan-American Copyright Convention. No part of this book may be reproduced, stored in a retrieval system, or transmitted in any form, or by any means, electronic, mechanical, photocopying, recording, or otherwise, without prior permission of the publisher.

04   03   02   01   00   99   5   4   3   2   1

Published by Allworth Press
An imprint of Allworth Communications
10 East 23rd Street, New York, NY 10010

Cover design by Douglas Design Associates, New York, NY

Page composition/typography by SR Desktop Services, Ridge, NY

ISBN: 1-58115-014-8

Library of Congress Catalog Card Number: 98-72764

Printed in Canada

To Kimia—

Hold me up to the light; you will see poems.
Hold me in the dark; you will see light.

Contents

Preface xi

1. The Author's Way 1
The Best Darn Job in the World, and Travel Too
Set Your Own Hours
Freedom from Bosses and Middle Managers
The Chance to Help Others
Research Makes You Learn Something New Every Day
If You Like to Tell Stories, Article Writing May Be for You
Writing Can Be an Adventure

2. The Article: Definitions and Types of Markets 11
Article Genres
The General Interest Article
The Art-of-Living Article
The Academic Article
The Technical Article
The Celebrity Profile
The Travel Article
The Family Article
The Current Events Article
The How-to Article
The Health and Fitness Article
The Religious and Inspirational Article
The Computer and High Tech Article
The Self-Help Article
The Business Article

3. Where to Find Ideas for Articles 29
Ideas Are All Around You
Reading Your Way to Article Ideas
The Internet: A Smorgasbord of New Ideas
The Idea Folder: A Treasure Trove of Your Best Ideas
Reliable Sources of Article Ideas

4. Preparation: Getting Set to Write 41
Useful Tools of the Trade
What Computer Systems and Software Are Right for You?
The Best Writing Routine for You
Writing Methods of Some Contemporary and Famous Writers
The Master Key to Writing Success

5. Get It on Paper: Forty Ways to Get Started 49

**6. How to Organize Your Article: The Five _W_s
and Other Techniques** 59
Who?
What?
When?
Where?
Why?
The Outline: Is it Necessary?
The Parsing Method

7. Titles Catch the Reader's Attention 67
Titles Are Headlines
Examples of Strong Titles
How to Create Fresh Titles
Titles Lead to Articles
Titles Are Fun to Write
Key Points to Remember
Practice Exercises

8. The Lead Is Critical 73
Types of Leads
How to Write Better Opening Paragraphs
What to Do When Nothing Works
Practice Exercises

9. An Article Is a Series of Paragraphs 81
The Paragraph: Content and Structure
Four Sample Paragraphs

Like a String of Pearls, Paragraphs Linked Together Build Articles
Transitions Between Paragraphs
Examples of Paragraph Transitions
Heavy-Duty and Easygoing Paragraphs
Points to Remember
Practice Exercises

10. How to Create a Midsection That Doesn't Sag 89
Elements of a Midsection
Anecdotes
Where to Find Anecdotes
Basic Tips for Using Anecdotes
Examples
Sources of Examples
Numbers Add Weight to Articles
Quotations
Sample Reports
Comparisons or Contrasts
Should You Add Photographs, Sidebars, or Graphics?
Improving the Body
Points to Remember
Practice Exercises

11. Interviews Add Credibility to Your Words 103
Advantages of Interviewing
How to Conduct an Article Interview
Points to Remember
Practice Exercises

12. How to Sell Your Articles 109
A Few Words Concerning Editors
Know Your Markets
How to Test Your Ideas before Submitting Them
Submissions to Editors and the Editorial Process
Query the Editor First
How to Write a Query Letter with Impact
Sample Query Letters
Submitting Your Article: Paper, E-mail, or Floppy Disk?
A Little Luck Never Hurts
Selling Your Articles to Overseas Markets
Disadvantages of Selling to Overseas Markets
Advantages Outweigh Disadvantages

How to Deal with Rejection Letters
Words of Advice
A True Story: The Article That Sold on Its Forty-ninth
Submission

13. Writing Articles for the Internet 129
Selling Your Articles to the Online Market
Online Queries: Necessity or Waste of Time?
Building Your Digital Writing Portfolio
Once Published, Take Advantage of Your Newfound Fame

14. Orphan Articles, Filler Articles, and Miscellaneous Writing Venues 137
Orphan Articles
Other Venues for Articles
Public Relations Writing
Advertising Copywriting
Greeting Card Ideas
Filler Money

15. Living the Writer's Life 143
Write Something New Every Day
Being Your Own Boss
A Few Words of Encouragement

Appendix A: FAQs 147

Appendix B: Sample Articles 153
Some Tips Toward More Effective Practice
Raising the Bar
The Law of Karma
The Six Most Common Barriers to Developing an Effective
Web Business Strategy
Dare to Always Have a Dream
The Power of Praising Employees
Those Magic Referrals
How to Write a Classified Ad
The "Groundhog Day" Phenomenon: A Lesson in Customer
Convenience

Suggested Reading List 195

Index 199

About the Authors 209

Preface

The wonderful thing about writing is that practically everything you do and everywhere you go can be subjects for articles. Life is filled with unsolved mysteries, heartwarming memories, tales of grief, stories of courage, legends, and other vivid moments that are worth talking about again and again. An article is a tale well told. An article takes one tiny story and magically brings it to life for the masses.

This book will help you realize your inherent power for creative expression by showing you how to transform your bright ideas—and the myriad tales floating around in your head—into salable articles.

How to Write Articles That Sell is a practical and inspirational handbook that will guide you through the mysteries of researching, writing, and selling freelance articles to magazines, newspapers, and the Internet. You'll get advice on how to pick a topic, how to tailor articles to a particular market, how to query editors, and how to make money from emerging new markets such as the Internet. Along with a useful question-and-answer section located in the appendix of this book, you will also learn tricks of the trade, how to conduct successful interviews, and how writing can be a way of life. Above all, this book will inspire you to continue in this fascinating craft.

How to Write Articles That Sell can show you how to make a contribution as an article writer and build a rewarding future at the same time. More power to you as you embark on the great adventure of creating and selling your ideas and words. Welcome to the creative and stimulating world of article writing!

—————✥—————

All of us are on a magical journey to find out what is related to what and why. As wordsmiths, it is our pleasure to connect the dots of life—filling in the blank spaces with beautiful, glorious words. Amazingly, it is within our power to touch the human spirit with mighty pens. Within us lies the ability to motivate, anger, inspire, liberate, frustrate, humiliate, expose, explore, delve deeply, unearth, uncover, instigate, emancipate, and invigorate. As artists and tellers of tales, the entire world is our canvas. As Erica Jong once said, "We are ink and blood and all the things that make stains." We, the writers, bleeding for our craft. It's been said that great things come to those who are willing to put it all on the line—to make the sacrifices others are unwilling to make. It is a reward that must be earned—one article, one poem, one short story or novel at a time. Never forget that.

—JON AND L.P.

The Author's Way

Statistics show there are thousands of possible vocations to choose from in today's world; but finding one that is fulfilling and offers the most potential for growth—with the least amount of aggravation—is a real challenge. It's like what Butch Cassidy said to the Sundance Kid, "Ranching is murder." Trouble is, the only vocation Butch and Sundance could tolerate was robbing banks. It's too bad they never tried article writing, the best job of all.

In the pages and chapters ahead, we will show you why professional article writing, for profit, is one of the best ways to go with your energy, talent, and time. Think about it: Your free time is worth money! Most of those who send an occasional article to a magazine or newspaper are happy if it sells and welcome the extra money. Right now, wherever you are, your mind contains information for potential articles. What do we mean by this? Simply that there are bound to be at least a few areas and subjects about which you know more than most. With a little time, and perhaps research or interviews, you could turn this information into salable articles.

The Best Darn Job in the World, and Travel Too

In professional article writing for profit, you can live anywhere you wish, work for yourself, and potentially see your income rise from year to year, in spite of almost unbelievable competition.

People who write articles are creators, or artists, if you like. Need we tell you that one of life's greatest joys is the ability to create something that pleases you and others as well? Those who can do this are rich, in the true meaning of the word.

So what are the rewards? First, a byline, which is your name printed in a magazine or newspaper as the writer of the article. After seeing their first bylines in print, many writers become hooked on writing as a way of life, and never look back.

What else? Another reward is payment for your articles. It's very pleasing to open an envelope from an editor, see a check fall out, and realize your article has been purchased and will sooner (or later) be published in a newspaper, magazine, newsletter, or other print publication. If you have access to the Internet, you might also be able to sell your articles to online newsletters, 'zines, or other electronic destinations.

A third reward—and it's important—is the plain satisfaction of knowing that your articles are helping, entertaining, and influencing others.

Let's take a look at each of these three basic rewards of professional writing. Imagine all the print ads you see in a month. Have you ever seen a byline on an ad? Copywriters don't get bylines. Of course, *they* know they wrote the ads; but they receive no public acknowledgment. The bottom line is this: Byline credit is a nice plus for the professional article writer.

The checks you receive for accepted articles may be small, medium, or large. It depends on the nature of the article, its length, if any photos were provided, and what value the magazine or publication places on it. The scope and distribution of the publication also effect the size of the payment; obviously, a brand-new magazine with a specialized audience will not be in the position to cut large checks.

The nice thing about article checks is the fact that they can add up. If you sell enough articles in a given month, or quarter, the sheer number will add up to a pleasing total. Some hardworking writers manage to sell twenty or more articles in a single month!

Become an article writer and, over the years, you will reach a great many people—your readers. Each magazine or newspaper has a different circulation. One religious magazine, for example, has a national circulation of one million readers. Obviously, in a year's time, the number of people you reach with your writing can be enormous.

Then add up a twenty-, thirty-, or forty-year writing career and all the sales made in that time, plus the circulation of all the publications, and you will quickly realize that article writers reach many millions of readers in the course of their lives.

Here are a few of the specific ways an article writer helps readers:

- Informs them about current events, the arts, matters of consumer interest, and hundreds of other subjects
- Entertains them with adventure, travel, humor, and action writing
- Inspires them with touching, true accounts, human-interest stories, and tales of personal triumph
- Stimulates their thinking with provocative and revealing articles
- Teaches them how to do something, reach a goal, start their own business, or improve their personal lives

Set Your Own Hours

Writers determine what hours of the day, evening, late night, or weekend they will devote to article writing. The individuals who choose this work, which can become a way of life, plan and keep their own schedules. Both authors of this book have worked on articles at just about all times of the day and night.

Those who shy away from writing complain they don't have the time, but real writers have no problem with this and write whenever and as often as they wish. Even the busiest person, holding down a non-writing position during the week, has the weekends to turn out a variety of articles. All manner of articles have been written on weekends.

An article writer has the choice of when to do the work. No nine-to-five restrictions here. If the words don't come at one writing session, you simply try again at another time. This freedom of time is one of the key advantages of professional article writing.

Freedom from Bosses and Middle Managers

What other business or profession allows you to be your own boss and work when and where you want? Writing articles for profit provides the opportunity to make more money each year and know the great joy of being your own person.

Life should be more than just earning a living. How a person earns his money can make a great difference in the quality of his life. What good is a nice paycheck if one hates the work? Those who love the work they do are the blessed and happy people in this world.

This freedom, however, is a double-edged sword. To some, it will bring pure joy. To others, it may bring misery. Countless millions may be better off taking orders from a manager or supervisor. It's a matter of knowing yourself. With the freedom of article writing comes the responsibility to put in the time, to get the work done, and to send the articles off to market. Many people might be tempted to abuse this freedom; to goof off, to quit after lunch, or to hit the golf course.

"Know thyself" is worthy advice that should be heeded by anyone thinking of entering the ranks of professional writers. If you are used to, or need, a supervisor to tell you what to do all day, then article writing is probably not for you. The only thing you can do is experiment and try to discover if you could handle this freedom wisely. An article writer must be true to the calling and make her free time count.

The Chance to Help Others

A writer may never know how many readers his articles have helped. If he could personally track each article and discover what it meant to its readers, the result could be inspiring.

An article may cheer the spirits of readers, help them find better jobs, teach them to be more disciplined people, persuade them to take action, or inspire them to run for political office. Art-of-living articles help people cope with various problems and get more out of life.

Not all readers of a given magazine or newspaper will see your article, but the combined circulation adds up. Over the course of a long writing career, many millions will probably read your words. That's communication on a wide scale.

Today's era of the Internet also impacts and extends the chance to help others. Thousands of published articles are now available via the Internet. If someone mentions he forgot to read a recent article in *People, Reader's Digest, Success Magazine, Wired,* etc., he can log online, visit a magazine's Web site, and, in many instances, print out the article he needs. What this means is that even more people will be reached and helped by your articles.

Research Makes You Learn Something New Every Day

Many an author, sooner or later, discovers what a joy research can be. In fact, some writers prolong the research stage because of the intense interest and pleasure it often provides.

Take for example the writing of travel articles. Those writers who specialize in this area learn a great deal about the geography, people, and cultures of their subjects. Over a period of years, through publishing many articles, a travel writer accumulates an enormous amount of knowledge about the history, customs, and way of life of these people and places.

One author of this book, L. P. Wilbur, once did a travel article about an Englishman, John Merrill, who spent a remarkable ten months walking around the coastline of England, Wales, and Scotland. Merrill's amazing seven-thousand-mile adventure consumed, required, wore out, or used up the following:

- Three pairs of boots
- Hundreds of gallons of milk
- Thirty-three pairs of socks
- A thousand bars of chocolate
- Sixty pounds of equipment

Merrill met hundreds of people on his walk and was interviewed by the local press, radio, and television along the way.

A writer working on a travel article about England, Wales, or Scotland would have thus found an excellent source of information in Merrill. By interviewing him, all manner of facts and information could be gleaned for travel articles about these countries. Excellent research material is gained from such interviews, because the writer is talking to an eyewitness.

Any city, region, town, or country may spark a desire to write. L. P. Wilbur still remembers being in Majorca, Spain, while serving in the United States Navy. A group of people from his ship took a one-day tour of this beautiful, sunny island (in January) and were enchanted by it. In mid-afternoon, at the highest point of the island, they were admiring the view of the ship in the harbor below when they saw an Englishman with a cane strolling toward them.

He greeted the sailors and told them that he and his wife had been in Majorca for eight months, after arriving for what was supposed to be a brief visit. He said they were renting an entire villa for the unheard of low price (at the time) of thirty pounds. "A maid comes each day and cooks all the meals, does all the cleaning and other chores, for fifteen pounds (about $22). I can't get my wife to leave," said the man, "and wonder if we'll ever see England again." What a tantalizing seed for a travel article this chance encounter provided!

The same holds true for other types of articles. You never know where you will unearth a tidbit of information, or come across a fascinating story that will inspire an article. Major holidays have been the springboard for many articles; take New Year's, for example. While doing research on this celebratory day, many writers learn things they never knew before:

- New Year's Day is the oldest holiday. Both civilized and primitive peoples have marked its arrival with some kind of festival, ritual, or custom.

- The Babylonians were believed to have observed New Year's Day as early as 2600 B.C.

- From the overflowing of the Nile River during the summer, the ancient Egyptians knew that the new year was at hand.

- Early American Indians got their new year's clue from the ripening of acorns.

Become an article writer and you, too, will have peculiar and fascinating facts at your fingertips. It's a major fringe benefit of professional article writing.

If You Like to Tell Stories, Article Writing May Be for You

Never forget this basic tenet of writing: Truth is stranger, and often much more fascinating, than fiction. If you like to tell stories—true stories—then article writing may well be the pathway for you.

Most readers would rather explore the world of nonfiction—what is actually happening, both locally and internationally. Think about it. In America alone, consider all the events in each of fifty states in a single day. You will never run out of stories if you cast your lot with nonfiction articles.

Case in point: Some years ago, L. P. Wilbur climbed aboard an Amtrak train, then known as the "Empire Builder." It was reportedly one of the best train rides in America, leaving Chicago in mid-afternoon and arriving in Seattle, Washington two days later.

What a train ride it was! He went through Milwaukee, Minneapolis (late the first night), on through Fargo, Billings, and eventually over the continental divide and into Portland, finally arriving in Seattle. During that trip all manner of ideas for potential articles became clear. Each town provided fresh inspiration. Looking out the window in the darkness of Minneapolis, L. P. conjured up an article about all the lakes in the area, and another about the underground shopping center located there.

Passing through Fargo suggested an article about the oil industry, focusing on the many strikes that had recently taken place there. Montana naturally brought George Armstrong Custer to mind, and the battle of Little Big Horn. Was Custer really crazy, as some articles and documentaries have indicated? Did the Indians of the Black Hill area, in South Dakota, blame him for the influx of so many settlers? More food for thought, and more grist for the article mill.

And it wasn't just the sights, zipping past the Pullman car's windows as the train flew down the track, which inspired L. P. His fellow passengers also gave him ideas. One day, a group of travelers were in the dining car, eating dinner and chatting about trains versus planes and automobiles. Everyone at that table preferred train travel above any other method, and couldn't understand why the locomotive industry didn't—and still doesn't—do a better job of promoting its advantages. L. P. started thinking about how Amtrak could go about improving its image and making itself more competitive, and this led to a meditation about how many people could really benefit from tuning up their presentational skills. These thoughts spawned an article called "Sharpen Your Competitive Edge." There is no question that travel stimulates story ideas.

Sometimes one's personal travails can provide the spark for an article. An attractive young woman once decided to share the story of her move to a strange city in an attempt to make a new start after a failed marriage. This led to an article entitled "Dare to Make a New Beginning."

Starting over is an important subject that can be approached in a variety of ways. In researching "Dare to Make a New Beginning," the young woman came across many examples of individual courage in action. However, for every person who dares to make a fresh start, millions are afraid to take the plunge.

Autobiographical essays can make great articles. Way back in 1571, Michel de Montaigne, a thirty-eight-old French nobleman, left public life and found the value of a new beginning. He situated himself in his country home and spent the rest of his life writing. The subject he chose to write about was himself. He called his works "essays," meaning that they were experiments in a new kind of literature. A fresh start and a whole new career thus enriched the world, along with Montaigne's own life.

Nowadays, the autobiographical essay is a very popular form. One need only look at the number of columnists who, on a daily basis, regale newspaper readers with stories and observations from their own lives. From the thoughtful, self-reflective reveries of Anna Quinlan, to the hyperbolic, self-mocking tirades of Dave Barry, all kinds of autobiographical essays appeal to today's readers. You, too, may find recounting your daily thoughts and actions to be rewarding.

Children are great catalysts for story ideas. A visit to a video store, where little ones as young as seven or eight years old were checking out videos that contained sex, violence, foul language, and adult situations, led to a published article entitled "Who's Baby-sitting Your Children?" The article was a wake-up call to parents who, either out of lack of concern or neglect, were allowing their children to choose the type of entertainment they could bring into the home. Unfortunately, in today's busy world, many parents don't bother to ponder the long-term consequences of exposing their children to inappropriate media. First Lady Hillary Clinton likes to say it takes a village to raise a child; a well-written article is one way to get the village's attention.

The story possibilities are everywhere, if you train your mind to be alert for them. A two-day visit to San Francisco, and the highlight of interviewing five executives of emerging Internet companies, led to an article titled "Start-ups versus Start-agains: The Battle of the Net Economy." Facts learned about the business practices of these online upstarts were very interesting. The companies had hundreds of computer programmers, designers, marketing strategists, writers, and production managers devoting thousands of hours to building Web sites, which were to be utilized as serious vehicles of commerce and communication for their respective firms.

Most of the employees were young (under twenty-five years old), lived in the surrounding area, and worked extremely long hours (twelve to eighteen hours per day). A few dedicated (or insane) employees never left their offices during deadlines, preferring to roll out sleeping bags on the floor next to their desks—catching three or four hours of sleep before they returned to their tasks. Talk about loving your work!

Writing Can Be an Adventure

Remember the words of Rhett Butler when he told Scarlett he was leaving her and wished to find peace and contentment again in his life? Scarlett asked him, "Where will you go, what will you do?" Rhett replied at once, "The world is filled with many places and many things, many people. I won't be lonely!"

Become an article writer and you, too, will never be lonely. Every day, week, month, and year will be filled with adventures into the world of the true, the world all around you, even now. You will come to think of yourself as a seeker of truth, a storyteller of a thousand events, places, people, observations, and ideas.

Above all, you will inform, guide, uplift, cheer, convince, persuade, entertain, and inspire millions of readers here, perhaps in Europe, and, quite possibly, all over the world, via syndication of your work. Your articles will make a difference and enrich the lives of others. Not a bad way to spend your time, ability, and energy!

CHAPTER 2

The Article: Definitions and Types of Markets

Consider this definition of an article from a highly respected literary agent: "The magazine article is a nonfiction piece with a beginning, middle, and an end. It should leave the reader with a theory or conviction about a related set of facts, or with an emotional attitude towards a related set of facts, or with a belief in the truth or falsehood of one or more statements or theories based upon a set of related facts."

Funk and Wagnall's *New Standard Dictionary of the English Language* says that an article is "a brief composition as in a serial publication," while the *Random House Dictionary* states it this way: "An article is a factual piece of writing on a specific topic."

We offer this definition of an article: An article is a focused angle on a subject. Take the subject of travel, for example. If a writer tried to write a general travel article, it would be like trying to swim the Atlantic Ocean. It's too wide, too broad! A segment of the overall subject must be selected—the writer goes for a focused angle on travel. To do this, he looks for a segment of the subject that he can manage. How about "The Best Tourist Bargain in London"? You must admit that that is more interesting than simply "travel."

In other words, an article must have a narrow enough focus. The lack of focus explains why a great many articles are rejected. Try to cover too large a subject and the odds increase greatly that an editor will pass on it.

There are three simple steps to achieving this focus. First, decide on your overall subject. Subjects for articles are endless. Some examples are: marriage, politics, money, real estate, music, investing, fishing, television, Canada, California, taxes—the list is endless. Make a list of the overall subjects that interest you and what you think you would like to write about.

Second, narrow the subject to a central idea or point of focus. One good way to do this is to ask yourself what interests you about the subject. It is far better to pick some part of the subject that you find curious, intriguing, or fascinating.

Third, simply create a title by experimenting with ideas and phrases. Write them down until one hits you as just what you want.

The authors of this book have long been fans of old popular songs, so it was easy to narrow down the topic "music" for a freelance article. Since we were intrigued by the way in which old songs affected people's memories and emotions, our angle concerned nostalgia. We probed our memory for what it was like to suddenly hear an old familiar song at various times—shopping in a supermarket, driving on the freeway, or riding in an elevator in an office building, for example. The resulting article ran close to twenty-five hundred words, and the final title was "Funny How the Great Old Songs Get to You."

Here is another example. You hear a lot these days, both from people and the media, about road rage. Years ago, before all the media attention, the idea for an article hit L. P. Wilbur while shaving: Why not write about rudeness on the roads and highways? The idea grabbed attention and was published in *California Highway Patrol* as "Rudeness on the Road." Here is the lead, or first paragraph:

> One of us has to go—man or the automobile. With more than 60,000 Americans losing their lives in motor accidents every year, it's obvious that present safety measures are not doing the job. While there are a number of standard causes for auto accidents, such as drunk driving, one cause is seldom discussed: Rudeness. It's doing more than its share of the killing on the roads.

What kinds of ideas make the best articles? It's a good question. An idea that interests you will often interest others and result in a fine article, but this isn't foolproof. There are times when things just don't gel; when beautiful article ideas just don't work out the way you planned. Maybe it wasn't the right idea for you; perhaps it required more time than you could devote. All in all, however, you have to trust your gut. Writer Nancy Davidoff Kelton advises writers to "trust ideas that stir you." If you are genuinely interested and excited about an idea, you will usually do much better writing it.

Especially if you're new to the writing business, you should remember: Ideas are the least of a writer's worries. Most experienced writers have a wheelbarrow of ideas; the sticky part is selecting the right ones, the best ones, and developing them . . . getting them all down on paper.

Article Genres

In *Writing the Creative Article*, Marjorie Holmes presents an interesting definition: "The creative article is neither fact nor fiction, though it contains elements of both. It is any article in which ideas are more important than facts, and whose purpose is to help, teach, amuse, move, or inspire."

There are different ways of classifying articles, but consider the following list of types of articles:

- The general interest article
- The art-of-living article
- The academic article
- The technical article
- The celebrity profile
- The travel article
- The family article
- The current events article
- The how-to article
- The health and fitness article
- The religious and inspirational article
- The computer and high tech article
- The self-help article
- The business article

The General Interest Article

The classification "general interest" covers a wide range of subject matter. It includes daily-life concerns that would attract a large number of readers. Some examples of general interest titles are "My Husband's Mother Was the Other Woman," "The Inflation Fighters," and "The Titanic Afloat in the Public's Imagination."

Here are some tips on writing the general interest article:

- Think about likely subjects with strong human-interest appeal. Subjects like money, happiness, and success have universal appeal. You should try to focus on a specific aspect of the subject.

- Make a list of what is going to be of major interest and concern to people in the early years of the twenty-first century. Such a list might include:

  —Energy conservation
  —Global warming
  —Increased competition among colleges and universities for new students
  —New inventions
  —High tech
  —Investing and the stock market

- Examine the possibilities of subjects that irritate, excite, intrigue, inform, convince, challenge, and entertain readers. After reading a newspaper item, L.P. became interested in writing about the subject of achievement. He sent a query letter to an editor, and the result was a published, fifteen-hundred-word article entitled "The Satisfaction of Achievement."

- Let your mind explore the fascinating array of possible subjects. You can lie awake at night for hours just letting all the potential ideas flash through your head. Pick a subject out of a hat and chances are that you could write a general interest article about it.

- Ask yourself what subjects seem currently neglected. If your article covers subject matter that is off the beaten track, it can sometimes increase your chance of making a sale. For example, one alert writer discovered there wasn't much written on merry-go-rounds (at that time). She wrote an article on them and their changes over the years, doing some of her research by visiting numerous amusement parks.

- Dawn B. Sova, in her book *How to Write Articles for Newspapers and Magazines*, offers a sensible suggestion for getting ideas for the general article. "Observe the people and places around you."

- Remember that your perspective, or angle, on your subject is almost as important as the information you present. Everybody likes to laugh; if you have a humorous take on your material, or if you can present it in an amusing light, you may increase your article's general appeal.

The Art-of-Living Article

This type of article is often homespun and creative, offering readers useful advice and tips on living happier and more productive lives. Take depression as a subject. Many articles have offered advice or hints on overcoming this downcast feeling of the human spirit.

Writer Dawn Sova suggests reading the personal and classified ads for ideas. Nancy Kelton's advice fits this and other article categories as well: "ideas, like love and most good things, appear when we least expect them, not when we demand they should."

The Academic Article

The term "academic article" can mean an article in a journal published by a college, university, or institution. These journals tend to specialize in some specific aspect of history, the sciences, literature, visual arts, theater, etc. While such publications can be fonts of information for novice writers, they usually print the works of authors who are experts (and have advanced degrees) in their particular fields.

However, general interest magazines and daily papers frequently publish articles about educational and academic developments. Writing this type of academic article might be right up your alley. One very helpful suggestion for this category is to keep up with new programs, seminars, and conferences in the academic world. What issues seem to be at the forefront? Some writers actually sit in on selected university classes to keep a current feel for this kind of article.

The Technical Article

Unless you are an expert on a technical subject, or have the ability to understand such material, you might find this category tricky.

However, some gifted writers have the talent and ability to communicate complicated or technical facts in a simplified manner. A warning is in order, though: Don't take on a subject that is over your head.

The Celebrity Profile

The celebrity profile is a type of article that may sell quickly, depending on the subject and what the article reveals. Arranging for interviews with celebrities takes time, effort, and patience; but it can be done. Try to see celebrities when they are in your area. Ask for an interview. In many cases, writers with celebrity contacts have an edge. After all, being able to get to celebrities makes such articles possible.

The daughter of friends writes a weekly column for a small-town newspaper where she lives in Iowa. When *The Bridges of Madison County* was filmed nearby, and Clint Eastwood came to town with a Hollywood crew, this young woman got an interview with Clint for her column. On occasion, celebrities may come to you. However, most of the time a writer will have to go to the celebrity, often going through a personal manager to do so.

Sometimes, you can go to watch a celebrity speak or entertain live. After the program or performance is over, you can sometimes go backstage or up to the front of the hall and ask a few questions. A request for an interview with the celebrity may or may not be granted. Request an interview for a future date if the celebrity will remain in town some days longer. If you don't ask celebrities for interviews when they are in your region, you may never get one. If you do ask, they may say no; but, hey, at least you tried.

The plus of asking for an interview directly is you can bypass the personal manager or public relations assistant, who may never permit you to reach the celebrity. Some years ago, L. P. Wilbur met the late Jeanne Dixon after she spoke at a meeting in Washington, D.C. She went into a side room, where she greeted those who wished to meet her or ask questions. Mrs. Dixon answered a number of questions and later sent a photo and other support material to L.P. from her Washington business address. That material and the questions she answered provided enough information for an article. The photo was an extra bonus.

Another tip for getting an interview is to write to the agent or manager of the celebrity. An interview may be granted, if it fits into the celebrity's schedule. If you are granted an interview, you will have to travel to where the celebrity lives, or visit the set where he or she is currently working.

Don't rule out the idea of a telephone interview. It may be possible to get a lot of information over the phone. Of course, talking to a celebrity on the telephone may not be as thrilling as sitting within touching distance of that person. But writers take what they can get.

Every year there are directories published that list the personal or business addresses of famous people. Take these with a grain of salt. It's possible that you can write some of them directly and request interviews, but in reality most celebrities will ignore your inquiry. It's not that they don't want to be interviewed, but rather that they fear the unknown. There are too many crackpots in society today who threaten the health and well-being of a well-known person. It's no wonder that so few of them open themselves up to potentially dangerous or unpleasant situations.

Tabloids such as the *Star*, *National Enquirer*, *Globe*, and others buy a lot of celebrity articles, but again, you need some news angle, something fresh about the person. Your personal slant, gained from experience doing other (noncelebrity) profiles can bring this to the article. Writer Bob Schultz, with over 175 published articles to his credit, says "the skills I have acquired interviewing a small-town mayor or the local handwriting analyst are the same skills I've used to interview celebrities."

One other thing to remember, if you decide to pursue celebrity interviews. Nowadays if a VIP or star has something to promote, such as a book, or a film, he or she will be more accessible than usual. Interviews are one of the ways in which celebrities get the word out—get a buzz going—about their pet projects. (Of course, it is even more useful if you can claim that you are writing on assignment, and if you can name the magazine where the interview will be published.)

Why not try this category, if you find it appealing? (For more information about the interview process, see chapter 11.)

The Travel Article

Millions of people dream of being able to travel but rarely get to because of any number of reasons. The only way they have to participate is to read travel articles. Imagine how many would drool over Merrill's fabulous coastline walk. In fact, travel articles of all types bring vicarious pleasure to many a reader. What fires the armchair traveler's imagination is hearing about how someone actually did it, someone who had the daring, imagination, and determination to make an adventurous idea become a reality.

Travel articles fan and feed the desire to get away from it all. Millions have trouble coping with the problems of modern life. They seek escape, if only for a few weeks. They also like the idea of a fresh start somewhere else, and that increases their interest in reading about other cities, national regions, or countries overseas.

Keep in mind that there are various travel article markets: airline magazines; trailer, camper, and recreational vehicle publications; the Sunday magazine, or special travel section, of every major newspaper in the country; Internet travel-destination Web sites; bus and train magazines; and hotel, motel, and resort publications.

One of the best ways to trigger a travel article is to start with the places you have seen yourself. Where have you been in your past—or recently—that might make an interesting article? Even a weekend trip to a nearby area can be turned into a good article. Don't overlook short trips.

Jon Samsel wrote a travel article for Americans looking to visit the country of Costa Rica. Here's his introduction:

> Close your eyes and picture yourself in paradise. Warm trade winds blowing through your hair, crystal blue-green waters, the sound of distant waves, lush volcanic islands and deserted moonlit beaches have you completely relaxed and at ease. Welcome to Costa Rica!

An introduction like the one above is successful because it appeals to the reader's visceral imagination. By evoking the sensory aspects of the environment—the feeling of wind, the view of the ocean, the sound of the waves—the writer helps the reader escape to utopia—if only for a few moments.

Travel articles often contain information about where to stay, hotel and transportation rates, directions for getting there, tourist attractions, geography, food, local customs—anything that makes the destination intriguing to the reader. But what about problems that crop up, like sickness, losing money or credit cards, getting lost, car trouble, all the rest? As writer Don McKinney suggests, "If something has posed a problem for you, it's almost certain it's caused problems for others." Articles that help readers avoid bad luck or pitfalls are popular—and not just in the travel category.

You can take the trip, get all the facts, write it up later, and then try to sell the article. Or you might try to sell an editor on the idea before you travel to find out what kinds of articles the travel editors want. An editor, for example, may have plenty of articles on Ireland; knowing this in advance could save you time and effort.

A number of top writers specialize in the travel field. Some write their articles while doing the actual traveling. Others gather material first and then write it up when back home. It takes experience, however, to sell regularly in this field. If travel interests you, keep this category in mind as a possible area of specialization.

The Family Article

The ties that bind—meaning the family—can yield any number of helpful articles. For example, parenting articles are in demand these days, and realistic solutions to family problems can lead you to many bylines under this category.

Articles to help parents cope with their children; material on family values; and thoughtful, inspirational pieces designed to offer direction for young adults are all in the spotlight. The need for such articles is probably without limit.

Ask yourself what issues are affecting families of today. Then research the subjects that particularly interest you and go from there, lining up any interviews that relate to your subjects. Try to obtain an assignment from a family magazine editor. Writer Ruth Duskin Feldman states that "professionals who write for magazines normally write on assignment. Writing on assignment means that all of your writing time is spent on remunerative activity."

The Current Events Article

Sports, musical, school, civic, political, and other events may all suggest possible articles to an alert writer. Say, for example, you hear about a class reunion held by your old high school or college. It's always interesting to re-meet people whom you haven't seen in years, and to learn what they are up to today. But such an event can also provoke a roller coaster of feelings—happiness, fear, self-doubt, tenderness, sadness. Having an emotional response to such a get-together is a common experience. If you were to attend your class reunion, you could write an article focusing not only on the factual aspects of the gathering, but also on these more personal responses. An article like "The Fun and Pain of Class Reunions" could have broad human interest, as well as local appeal.

In fact, almost every current event holds the seeds of article ideas, which might be developed into effective material. Editorial director and writer David Fryxell points out the variety of subjects that have led him to produce diverse articles: "I've written about small-town theatrical productions, turtle hunting, and little old ladies who collect glass bottles."

How about politics of the past, present, and future? What, for example, were the presidential politics of George Washington? Or Jefferson, Andrew Jackson, or other presidents?

Congressional elections take place every two years in America, and presidential politics heat up about every three years, because they start at least a year before the election. Think of all the stories involving the primaries, the campaign trail from each candidate's viewpoint, and the whole process of getting the people to go out and vote for the "right" candidate.

Remember, politics happen all over the world, not just in the United States. The political landscape—and the potential for article sources—is global. For example, many articles have appeared regarding the British monarchy and its future. Will the Prince of Wales one day be king? This subject is tireless and will continue to generate interest.

The current events market signals its importance and potential on a daily basis. Author Dawn Sova advises writers to "examine local and national concerns and also to consider an issue from different points of view." As an article writer, you could simply follow current events and never run out of material or markets for your articles.

The How-to Article

Thumb through almost any magazine or newspaper and you're sure to find one or more how-to articles. Editors buy this kind of article continually. They are often easy and fun to write. If you know how to do something—and do it well—there may be others who would benefit from your knowledge and skill. So why not inform them?

The how-to article alone offers you hundreds, if not thousands, of article possibilities. There are part-time and full-time writers constantly tapping this seemingly endless category. Some current published examples are "How to Stop Smoking for Good," "How to Cope with Blue Mondays," and "How to Find the Right Vacation for You."

A how-to article teaches and explains a process, system, or way to do something, and imparts information. Here is an excellent, proven method that is sure to bring you a dozen or more article ideas in the popular how-to category. First, read and study the universal wants and desires held by most people. They are:

- To be successful
- To be healthy
- To be safe
- To save time
- To make money
- To be creative
- To be popular
- To be clean
- To be confident

As you consider each of these universal wants, relate each desire to a possible how-to article.

If you pick a how-to subject that you, yourself, know a great deal about, then make full use of your authority on the subject. As writer Donald Murray suggests, "Early in your article, you should—briefly— establish your authority by revealing your connection to the subject, including some specific, accurate information that will persuade your reader that you know your subject and have the right to be heard and trusted."

The Health and Fitness Article

Interest in health and well-being has boomed. Millions have become almost obsessed with improving their lifestyles, eating more sensibly, and exercising regularly. Preventive medicine has become a cottage industry, with doctors presenting seminars and suggesting better ways of living today. Articles that cover a wide range of physical and mental concerns are in great demand. Nowadays, many newspapers devote at least one special section a week to health matters, and health is the raison d'être for magazines such as *Men's Health*.

Take vitamins as just one example. The vitamin industry has sky-rocketed and shows no hint of flagging. Millions are consuming handfuls of vitamins daily, while others swear they feel better than ever because of the multivitamins they take each day. Articles about the effect of vitamins are very popular.

One health problem that currently concerns us all is "burnout." Workers everywhere are much more aware today of its effects, such as fatigue, the feeling of helplessness, loss of sleep, too much alcohol, a low energy level, frequent illness, not caring about anything, and an overall feeling of being emotionally drained. One does not have to be a typical office worker to feel the effects of burnout. Mothers at home, volunteer workers, and self-employed people are all possible victims. Many of those suffering from burnout believe they can get over what is bothering them by eating, drinking, or smoking more. It just isn't true. An article that presented health strategies for over-coming burnout could be invaluable.

One expert on stress management has this to say about the burnout problem: "Work is healthy for you. It is stimulating and pro-vides exercise. The body is designed to do work. What is unhealthy about it is that we are being called upon more and more to do more—and do it more quickly, more efficiently in terms of cost." An article writer could explore how a more efficient, technologically advanced world actually increases human burnout.

You could also write about food in the health and wellness category. Eggs, for example, were reportedly taboo and "not good for you" for some time. This view has recently changed. Now eggs are again on the list of healthy foods. You might choose a specific food and write about its beneficial qualities.

The fact is, we live in a world where sickness, physical fitness, and mental well-being are touchstones for controversy and conversation. As long as there are broken hearts, dietary fads, lost souls, and dam-aged bodies, there will be a market for well-written informative health and wellness articles.

In the words of writer Ruth Duskin Feldman, your query on health, or other types of articles, "must show that your topic is timely, that it will 'turn on' the magazine's readers, and that you can deliver what you promise: a well-researched, well-written, pub-lishable article."

The Religious and Inspirational Article

The religious and inspirational article has become very popular, due to a renewed interest in religion, riding the crest of spiritual material like *Transformed by the Light, Illuminata, Embraced by the Light, Talking to God,* and others. Many people today are placing more emphasis on their faith and spiritual life. This means editors need more such articles.

Take prayer, for example. A great many articles have been written on this subject. Let's make it more specific and focus on thanking God in prayer. Is there an article there? Thanking God in prayer for the many blessings that come your way is one thing, but what about the sad and tragic things that happen? How can a person continue to believe when surrounded by adversity?

In his book *The Will to Believe,* Marcus Bach relates his conversation with a graduate student whose child had burned to death in a stove explosion the previous day. The author tried to help this student see the possibility of meaning in such a tragedy. Bach told the student that he didn't know why such a misfortune would take place between God and an innocent child: "But in answer to your question as to what religion, what faith can do for you, religion and only religion can provide you with a will to believe at that point where reason stands confounded." Millions of people all over the world have come to realize that life is more than working, eating, and sleeping. Our faith and spiritual life are very important and come to our aid when the storms of life overwhelm us.

You could specialize in this subject and never run out of material. In addition to monetary payments, you will receive intangible benefits. Your work will help readers to face their troubles, to cope with daily problems, and to become better parents. You may ease the pain of those who grieve for lost loved ones. Perhaps one of your articles will even save a life or inspire a reader to do some great thing. Articles create ripples and waves that spread out, touching many lives. The bottom line is, spiritual writing can change many lives for the better.

The Computer and High Tech Article

It is predicted that within the next year, over 300 million people will be on the Internet. If you are one of these Net users, you have access to myriad, diverse resources. With just a couple of keystrokes, you can access hundreds of thousands of Web sites, or communicate with people all over the world. Of course, computers and the Internet themselves offer many fascinating subjects for writers, and the large population of users guarantees an audience of readers. However, not every writer can turn this category into articles. If you know computers well, and keep up with the fast-changing high tech world, this type of article might be a natural for you. Such articles are in demand.

If you have a great idea for a technology article, don't just sit there—write it and sell it! That's what Jon Samsel did. He contacted the editor of Hewlett-Packard's popular online magazine, *e-business*, via e-mail, and pitched her three possible story ideas with a focus on technology. Two days later, the woman responded favorably to all three. One was ultimately chosen and three weeks later, an article entitled "Raising the Bar: Nine Ways to Improve a Business-to-Business Web Site" was published.

In addition to providing new subject matter and new markets for articles, the Internet is an incredibly useful tool for authors. The huge amount of information available online has streamlined the article writer's job tremendously—and made the task of researching a topic as enjoyable as writing.

The Self-Help Article

Millions of readers in all countries look for the self-help article and respond to them warmly. You will get more than just a check for each article written for this field; you will also derive a sense of satisfaction for having helped your fellow man.

When you're ready to try your hand at this type of article, think about the problems or difficulties you have solved and overcome in your own life. The odds are good that many who face similar problems could gain insight from your article.

Find out what other writers are offering in the self-help area. Then consider doing your own versions on the same subjects. L. P. Wilbur was once visiting with a supermarket owner and chatting at the checkout counter about life in general. The owner made the statement that he "could count the number of his real friends on the fingers of one hand." This suggested and led to a self-help article entitled "The Miracle of Friendship." The article was published in *Grit*.

Even if you decide to focus on another type of article, you might experiment by writing an occasional piece in this area. In most cases, you don't need a lot of research, interviews, or travel. You can often write this article in the comfort of your home.

Take the subject of time as another example. Just about everyone wants to get more from each day and squeeze more accomplishment, work, and achievement out of the clock. Thinking about this human desire led to a published article entitled "Ten Ways to Get More from Your Time." Here are two paragraphs from the article:

> First, keep in mind that the amount of free time most of us have is increasing as the years go by. Put this free time to better use, and you will automatically get more done.
>
> You may now have a regular plan for your free time. If not, get busy and devise one. Like the sign said on the plantation of John Wilkes in *Gone with the Wind*, "Do not squander time, for that is the stuff that life is made of."

The opening paragraph grabs the reader by speaking directly to him in an optimistic manner, suggesting that he has more free time than ever before. The second paragraph exhorts him to make good use of this time, and very positively states that a successful plan can be achieved.

The article goes on to show the reader how to make lunch hours count more, how to review each night what can be done the next day, and how to prioritize time. The overall tone is encouraging, suggesting that it is within the reader's power to become a skillful time manager.

What can help you a lot with such articles is to stay aware of the daily problems of life and what motivates people. Think of the simple, happy things about life, such as family, the beauty of a sunrise, the sound of a much-loved song on the radio, the value of good health. These can all lead you to a self-help article worthy of publication.

The self-help category also includes useful information like how to pack smarter, raise teenagers more successfully, find more sense of fulfillment, be a better neighbor, or appreciate animals more. You have no way of knowing how many readers will be helped by such articles, but your writing may change a lot of lives for the better. Not a bad way to spend some of your energy, ideas, and time.

The Business Article

Business articles cover a wide choice of possible material, including pieces on real estate, banking and finance, investments, marketing, advertising, management, career advancement, money-saving ideas, profiles on various companies and the executives behind them, and business conditions and problems overseas.

You will naturally have an edge here if you are currently connected with the business community. People you may know in various lines of business can be valuable interview sources, so don't overlook any likely possibilities in your own area.

Some examples of business articles are "Make Your Sales Calls Count," "Office Condominiums," "Buying Your First Real Estate Property," "The Art of Managing Others," and "Hottest Stock Market Tips of the Year."

Here are some tips on writing business articles:

- Keep up with what is being published weekly or monthly on national business trends in this country and overseas.

- Watch for new ideas or methods to improve business, increase profits, find good employees, and streamline productivity; editors often snap up this kind of article.

- Read leading business publications regularly, for example, the *Wall Street Journal, Fortune, Business Week, Forbes,* and others. Take notes on the business subjects or areas in which you already have knowledge or ability.

- Set up interviews with business leaders in your city or surrounding area. They are often excellent subjects for articles and usually receptive to being interviewed, if they can fit it into their schedules.

- Look over business bulletins and newsletters carefully. Attend business conferences and meetings with the idea of developing a number of business article ideas.

- Keep a steady flow of query letters going out to editors of business publications.

- Keep in mind that the material you use for one business article can be changed, expanded, or rewritten with a different slant and then sold to other business publications. What is helpful to one group of business people may be useful to several others as well.

One almost sure way to write a business article is simply to interview a manager in your town. Think of all the businesses in your surrounding area and start listing them. Then try to contact the managers by telephone, fax, e-mail, or snail mail (the U.S. Postal Service). Ask for an interview. You might also visit their offices and request an interview from their secretaries or receptionists. L. P. Wilbur once lined up an interview with a respected hotel manager. The finished piece was published in a leading business magazine.

Sometimes the information you obtain in an interview will work for other magazine markets. The hotel manager, for example, explained the list of ten values that guided his employees. Some of these values were "placing team success over individual success, committing to standards and achieving them, accepting accountability for actions, striving to increase profitability, implementing change to grow and improve, treating guests as individuals, and treating colleagues with dignity and respect." This list of values could spin off a number of effective articles.

If you are granted interviews with business managers, do your homework. Arrive with a planned list of questions to ask, which means you need to understand the nature of the business in order to come up with thoughtful questions.

As an article writer, you could spend your entire career just focusing and writing on business. There are thousands of business ideas floating around out there, in a variety of different industries and businesses. There are also a lot of different approaches to these subjects and areas. Sales and marketing alone is a vast industry that triggers a huge number of helpful, practical, and inspiring articles on a regular basis. All you need to do is select the businesses and industries you wish to cover. Then go for them.

More power to you if you chose the world of business to report on and cover. By staying informed and alert, you will always have plenty to write about. You will also make a contribution to the business community and help to keep the goods and services of a nation moving. It's a great category in which to find your home base and put down roots.

.

Where to Find Ideas for Articles

This chapter title implies that some sort of search is needed to uncover article ideas. That is not the case. Ideas for articles are not hiding or trying to be elusive. They are all around you.

"Like most freelancers, most of my ideas come from other magazines, television shows, and press releases," says writer Todd Krieger. "Occasionally, because I am on a mailing list or have a friend involved in some kind of project, I get advance notice about some new development, but most of the time I might read something somewhere or hear a snippet about something, and then I just follow it up to its natural conclusion—a story."

Ideas Are All Around You

One of the earliest lessons an article writer learns is the fact that ideas for new articles are everywhere.

The problem is choosing the right ones and deciding which are worth your time and effort to expand and complete. Few article specialists ever run out of ideas. Finding enough time to complete the ideas they select is the problem.

It's a bit like the statement made by Charles Laughton, the superb film and stage actor, who died in 1962. Laughton said it this way: "Whenever I go into a large library and see all the books I know I'll never have time to read, I wish I could live for a thousand years."

Many article writers feel the same way about their craft. They wish they could stick around much longer in order to write and complete more articles on the vast array of ideas that constantly bombard them.

L. P. Wilbur once spent an entire day at Crater of Diamonds, in Arkansas, looking for sparkling gems. In previous years, many diamonds had been found in this crater, which is now reportedly closed. Searchers paid a fee for the chance to spend the day looking, and some people were there on most days. A small shovel and pail were provided. It was a fun experience to spend that day turning up dirt in hopes of finding a diamond. A backache hit after several hours of bending over and digging, but hope of spotting a diamond was strong.

In previous years, about two hundred diamonds were found annually in the 78-acre crater, which was part of an 837-acre park. The largest diamond found since March 1972 weighed over three carats. Some twenty-four other diamonds discovered in later years were over one carat. The famous "Star of Arkansas" diamond was found at the crater by a Dallas housewife in 1956. The "Uncle Sam" diamond was discovered in 1924 and weighed, in the rough, a whopping 40.23 carats.

L.P. found no diamond but spent a wonderful day looking. The pail of small rocks, dirt, and pebbles yielded no gems, but it had been a great adventure. Experiences like these from a writer's life can provide the grist of a great article.

The writer's search for article ideas can be as exciting and romantic as L.P.'s Crater of Diamonds adventure—and probably more fruitful. Idea "gems" are all around you. Once you start making your way as a writer, you will be overwhelmed by the hundreds of ideas that will engulf you, whispering in your mind's ear. Sometimes the four-star ones will scream to be written and demand your time and attention, "Write me, not those other ideas!"

Reading Your Way to Article Ideas

L.P. had heard about the Crater of Diamonds in a story he read in a newspaper. Fascinated by all the tourists who had visited, and also by the many diamonds found over the years, he was determined to drive there one day from Memphis, and he did. Back home in Memphis, armed with historical information, photos of the crater, and notes about his own unique experience, he soon completed a new article.

This is a clear example of an article inspired by a newspaper story. In fact, any form of the printed word may spark an article idea. As contemporary writer Don McKinney points out, "Somebody once did a survey of freelance writers to find out where they got their ideas. Topping the list was reading."

With some experience behind you as an article writer, you will begin to notice how ideas from the printed page leap out at you. In time, you will learn to separate the higher quality ideas from the rest of the pack.

Whenever you spend time reading, be alert for potential new article ideas. Train your mind to be receptive and grateful for them. Reading time then becomes quality working time for an article writer. Don't ever view it as time wasted. In fact, most writers love to read and divide their time between writing and reading (when they aren't researching or interviewing). The two pursuits feed each other, providing a happy and rewarding way of life.

The Internet: A Smorgasbord of New Ideas

Talk about an idea bonanza! That is exactly what the ever-growing, vastly popular Internet offers today's writers. Combine one's own ideas plus those waiting on the Internet, and you get a small idea of enormous potential. As the early years of the twenty-first century unfold, this idea smorgasbord can only expand to offer even greater choice.

Case in point: On a recent Saturday morning, Jon Samsel logged onto the Internet in an effort to find some information on public transportation available in the San Francisco Bay Area. A search for "Bay Area Transportation" led to a Web site devoted to information on BART (Bay Area Rapid Transit). The site included daily transportation schedules, ticket information, and assorted links to various Bay Area services. Clicking on a hyperlink to another Web site devoted to local tourist attractions revealed a site that listed over a hundred points of interest in the northern California area. One of those included a link to an oceanfront bed-and-breakfast cottage. A quick visit to that site uncovered an interesting story. The bed-and-breakfast had recently reopened after an extensive remodeling effort.

Business was down and the bed-and-breakfast proprietors felt that the Web site was an innovative way to reach out to prospective visitors. Any number of articles could easily have been generated from this online find. Articles dealing with the sudden downturn in the bed-and-breakfast industry, how to market online, virtual vacations, Internet public relations, and so on.

Soul-strengthening accounts of individuals who discover spiritual values and find personal fulfillment can be unearthed online as well—although you may have to dig a little to uncover them. New media consultant and friend Charles Austin stumbled upon a deeply personal discovery while surfing the Internet one night. It's a tale that would never have been possible without the Internet as the medium of discovery. Charles was kind enough to share with us how it happened:

> I was working the Web today for one of my clients, when, as is often the case, I started spacing out and surfing. I did a search on Yahoo! for the name "Aussenberg," my family name, and it came up with eight "matches." I looked into one of them and it contained a list of dozens of people who were trying to find other people, including an Earl Aussenberg of Pittsburgh, PA, who was trying to find information about his ancestors in Cracow, Poland.
>
> Mind you, my folks have been dead for thirty years, I have no siblings, and virtually no contact with any of my family, which is very small and lives all over the country. I had never heard of Earl Aussenberg, but e-mail's so immediate and easy, I sent him the following:
>
> *Hi, Earl. I'm Charles Austin, but my birth name was Charles Aussenberg. My father was Moritz Aussenberg. He was born in Leipzig, Germany in 1898, and I know his parents had been born in Poland. Does this help in your search for relatives?*

Here is the response I received:

Dear Charles, I met your father when I was about 13. He went to Long Beach where we met your mother. Your father was a wonderful man. We even visited his furrier store. I remember he sent me a Ronson lighter when I graduated high school. I even believe I spoke with you on the phone when I was in New York, shortly after your father passed away. Didn't you or your mother play the piano?

I am very glad you saw my message from my posting, in Poland perhaps? Please tell about yourself, your family, and where you now live.

I am married to Laverne (same name as my sister) and we have three children, Evan 34, Jon 31, and Hilary 27. I am writing this quickly, because I am excited and I want to hear from you. I have wondered about you over the years and hope your life has been gentle.

    Please respond to me. And yes, your information did help!

Your cousin, Earl

You can probably see that this little story itself has the makings of at least one human-interest article. It is an uplifting tale that exemplifies small miracles in everyday life—rediscovery of long-lost relatives and connection to the family of man. It could easily be expanded into a heartwarming piece. The anecdote also illustrates what a powerful resource the Internet is; a man sitting at his computer, rather distracted and bored, accidentally stumbles upon something stimulating and meaningful. On the Net, hyperlinks between sites mean that information doesn't have to be looked at sequentially; the user can jump from place to place, until he discovers something wonderful, which is actually very similar to the way the human mind works when seeking inspiration. The information and interactivity of the Net will continue to spawn new ideas for the articles, books, movies, and new media storytelling of the next millennium.

The Idea Folder: A Treasure Trove of Your Best Ideas

Writer John Hunt says he has only "to turn to my computer file and scan the ideas waiting there. This method works well for me." John also says that he "gets ideas from ideas." This is a valid point. Ideas can spin off ideas, and this is why it's important to be selective.

    Some article writers keep a special file or folder of their new or current ideas. Then they simply open the folder and look through its contents to stimulate a new project. Others keep notebooks or maintain a file card system. On each card they jot down a thought, an intriguing fact culled from the newspaper, or a bit of overheard conversation. They then arrange the cards alphabetically, or group them together in related categories.

    Quite a few writers like a system of alphabetized file folders (here, of course, we mean the manila folders that go into an actual file cabinet, not just the electronic files on your computer). The advantage of such an arrangement is that one can put all the material (pictures, photocopies, scrawls on napkins, etc.) related to an idea together in one safe, easily located place. Writer Don McKinney offers a good suggestion: "Start a clip file. When you see an item in a newspaper or magazine that sparks your interest, clip it out and file it away."

Reliable Sources of Article Ideas

Here are some specific sources for a variety of topical article ideas:

Daily Newspaper

Every article writer should read the newspaper carefully. Most large-city newspapers are gold mines of ideas. Even local newspapers can yield fine ideas.

Television

Many alert article writers get some of their top ideas from simply watching the tube. *TV Guide,* just to name one market, is very receptive to new articles about television people and shows.

Magazines

You will find it helpful to regularly scan a variety of magazines. Here are some guidelines on how to watch for ideas:

- Read the articles that interest you most. A seed for a new piece may be waiting for you to spot it.

- Glance at ad headlines in magazines. Sometimes an article idea will leap out at you from ads.

- Look over the table of contents carefully. In this way, you can quickly see all the article subjects in a given issue. Ask yourself if you could do your own article on some of the same subjects. This will tell you whether or not the magazine is a potential market for your work.

- Read a wide number of magazines, or at least look them over.

Include such categories as the following:

- General Interest (*Reader's Digest, People*)

- Nutrition and Fitness (*Shape,* the *Natural Way, Fitness, Prevention, Walking Magazine*)

- Travel/Inflight (*Hemispheres, Islands, Traveler, American Way*)

- Teen and Young Adult Interest (*Tiger Beat, Seventeen*)
- Religious Topics (*Catholic Digest, Virtue, Hope Magazine, Grit*)
- Sports (*Golf Digest, Field and Stream, Sports Illustrated, Backpacker*)
- Business and Finance (*Forbes, Kiplinger's Personal Finance, Upside, Fast Company*)
- Child Care and Parental Guidance (*Working Mother, Family Circle, Parenting, Child*)
- Entertainment (*Entertainment Weekly, Soap Opera Digest, TV Guide*)
- Women's (*Vogue, Glamour, Allure, Elle, Latina, Woman's Day, McCall's*)
- Retirement (*Modern Maturity, Mature Years, Prime Times*)
- Music (*Hit Parader, Stereo Review, Opera News*)
- Photography (*Popular Photography, American Photo*)
- Military (*Off Duty Magazine, Military History*)
- Men's (*Maxim, Playboy, GQ, Men's Journal, Details*)
- Personal Computers (*Yahoo!, Internet Life, PC Gamer, Computer Currents, Wired, Information Week*)
- Food and Drink (*Gourmet, Bon Appetit, Cooking Light, Food and Wine*)
- Automotive and Motorcycle (*American Motorcyclist, Car and Driver, Motor Trend*)
- Science (*Technology, Astronomy, Final Frontier, Popular Science*)
- Juvenile (*Disney Adventures, Sports Illustrated for Kids, Barney*)
- Home and Garden (*Better Homes and Gardens, Home Digest, Garden Design*)
- Hobby and Craft (*Blade, Craftworks, American Woodworker, Crafts 'n Things*)
- Astrology and New Age (*Fate, New Age, Astrology Magazine,* the *Aromatic Thymes*)
- Regional (*Yankee, Midwest Living, Los Angeles, New York, Sunset*)
- World Affairs and Politics (*George, U.S. News and World Report,* the *Nation*)
- Bridal (*Modern Bride, Bridal Guide*)
- Art and Architecture (*Artist's Magazine, Artforum, Art in America, Architectural Digest*)

- Animal (*Horse and Rider, Cat Fancy, Dog World*)
- Nature and Conservation (*Discover, Smithsonian, Audubon, National Geographic, Earth*)
- Contemporary Culture (*Mother Jones, High Times, Curio, Utne Reader, Esquire*)

Books

Books offer a tremendous source of article ideas. Here are just a few of the many kinds of books available. Ideas for new articles may be found in any or all of them:

- Books on business subjects—real estate, stocks, banking, advertising, insurance, and management
- Religious books
- Self-help books on all manner of subjects
- Books on the history of nations and peoples
- Mysteries
- Historical novels
- Mystical and occult books
- Books written for teens and children
- Textbooks on academic subjects
- Adventure and suspense books
- Humorous books

Pamphlets and Bulletins from Government Agencies

To get on the mailing list for information on new government publications, write to the following address. Request that your name be added to the list of those who receive the titles and brief descriptions of new government publications. Send your request to:

Superintendent of Documents
U.S. Government Printing Office
Washington, DC 20402

Newsletters

The value of subscribing to newsletters is that they keep you up-to-date in a specific field. Most people don't have the time to discover the latest information in their fields; a newsletter provides the latest news, condensed for easy reference.

There are newsletters on stock guidance, investments in general, stamp collecting, political analysis, marketing, publishing, and many other areas. The Author's Guild in New York sends a newsletter to all its members. The Venice Interactive Community (VIC) sends its monthly newsletter via e-mail to over a thousand members, at the click of a mouse. Valuable article ideas may be gleaned from a variety of newsletters.

Here are some resources you might consider for researching and obtaining information on newsletters:

Guide to Encyclopedia of Associations: Geographic and Executive Indexes, Sandra Jaszczak, editor (Farmingham Hills, Mich.: Gale Research, 1998).

The Directory of Business Information Resources: Associations, Newsletters, Magazines, Trade Shows, Directories, Databases, Leslie MacKenzie (Lakeville, Conn.: Grey House, 1997).

Public Speakers

Ideas for new articles may come to you while listening to any number of public speakers. Your local paper may list upcoming speakers at various organizations; universities often publish a calendar of lectures open to the public on a monthly or by-semester basis.

Museums

These places are filled with interesting items, and any one of them could suggest an article. An example here is the famous Metropolitan Museum of Art in New York. It once led L. P. Wilbur to research Vincent van Gogh. Seeing some of his paintings in the museum on a rainy afternoon led to a published article.

Special Journals

The annual edition of *Writer's Market* lists many specialized journals dealing with a number of scientific and technical subjects, as well as the arts. A good way to use these journals for ideas is to visit the periodical department of any large university library from time to time. Most major university libraries have all, or most, of the leading journals. And thanks to the Internet, many well-known journals are now archived online.

Just about every field you can name, such as nursing, advertising, or medicine, has its own journal. Some examples are *Advertising Age*, the *New England Journal of Medicine*, *Journal of Property Management*, *Journal of Information Ethics*, *Journal of Court Reporting*, *Journal of Safe Management*, and the *Journal of Petroleum Marketing*.

Resources for professional journals include:

- *World Directory of Trade and Business Journals* (London: Euromonitor Publications Ltd., 1998)

- *Directory of Political Periodicals: A Guide to Newsletters, Journals and Newspapers*, Lynn Hellebust, editor (Washington, D.C.: Government Research Service, 1992)

- *The Author's Guide to Biomedical Journals: Complete Manuscript Submission Instructions for 250 Leading Biomedical Periodicals*, Mary Ann Liebert, editor/publisher (Larchmont, N.Y.: Mary Ann Liebert Publishing, 1996)

- *An Author's Guide to Social Work Journals*, Henry N. Mendelsohn (Washington, D.C.: National Association of Social Workers, 1997)

- *Index Guide to College Journals*, Suzanne Milton and Elizabeth Malia, (Lanham, Md.: Scarecrow Press, 1998)

Travel
One of the best ways to gain new article ideas is to hit the road. Travel and the stimulus of new surroundings often spark fresh new article ideas.

Motion Pictures
"One picture is worth a thousand words" is still true. Sometimes a film will give you a flash of inspiration.

Personal Experience
Your own memory is a remarkable computer that contains many top article ideas. To grasp the scope of this source, consider the following as potential article wellsprings:

- *Past experiences.* Events that happened to you in the past. Simply search your memory by going back in time mentally. Old jobs, summer vacations, school activities, things that frightened you, and other experiences are just a few possibilities that might stir up new article ideas.

- *Everyday life.* Your current daily life, including your present activities, interests, and situation.

- *Conversations with others.* Talk to people and pay attention to the conversations you overhear.

- *Future expectations.* What you expect for the future, including your goals, hopes, objectives, desires, and plans.

- *Your journal.* Author Marcia Yudkin firmly believes in the value of journal-keeping. "Besides the [discipline] of keeping a journal, you can discover topics worth writing about by noticing what interests others in your daily conversations."

Remember, as an author, you are in the idea business. Ideas are really your stock in trade. May many great ideas come your way in the months and years ahead!

—=>◆<=—

CHAPTER 4

Preparation:
Getting Set to Write

Many who consider writing articles reject the idea because they are unable to do it full-time. In truth, article writing is an ideal way to supplement your income—on a part-time basis.

In fact, it's better not to jump into article writing full-time. The writer's income is one that builds gradually in the beginning. By starting part-time, you have an excellent chance to learn how to write effective articles without financial pressure.

While a graduate student at Emory University, L. P. Wilbur started writing articles after classes. The writing fit the student and teacher lifestyle and provided variety for each day and the ongoing excitement of wondering what would sell, if anything.

Useful Tools of the Trade

A dependable computer or word processor is an absolute must for your writing. If you can't manage either, then use an electronic typewriter—if you can find one. Typewriters are obviously being phased out, and some day soon they will be viewed as antiques (as many already consider them).

Computer prices are dropping, and bargains can be found, especially at certain times of the year. In north Florida, for example, a name brand computer, monitor, and printer were recently advertised at retail for $1,200. Online Auctioneer (*www.auctionuniverse.com*) sells similar systems for under $1,000. And you can find used systems in your local area for even less. You may pay more for a laptop, but some writers prefer the mobility of being able to take their computer just about anywhere.

If you can type fairly well, and have a computer or word processor, you already have a key tool of the trade for writing articles. If you do not type well, don't let it stop you. Many a writer began that way. In a few months, your typing will come much more easily, and you'll be flying along on the keyboard in short order.

If you want to learn to type faster, consider taking a course, or perhaps some lessons. If you own a computer, there are a number of programs you can load that will teach you how to type. Mavis Beacon Teaches Typing, produced by and available through the software company Mindscape (*www.mindscape.com*), has taught over 6 million people how to type. Typing is like swimming: the more of it you do, the better you get. With some practice behind you, you should be able to increase your keyboard speed.

If you're a pen-and-legal-pad kind of writer—or if you just know in your heart of hearts that you will never be able to type well enough to feel comfortable doing so on a regular basis—have no fear. Write with your voice. Buy a tape recorder and describe your article as if you were reading the finished piece out loud. Don't worry about making mistakes along the way. You will make plenty of them. When you are finished, take your audiotape to a local transcription service. It may not be cheap to have your tape transcribed, but if you can afford it, you'll end up with a first draft that you can edit in your free time.

Can't afford a transcriber but like the idea of not typing? Perhaps you can't type at all due to a disability. Voice recognition programs now on the market allow computer users to "speak" to their computers and watch their words magically appear on-screen. One such program, Dragon Naturally Speaking, is available for under $100, and is purportedly 98 percent accurate in translating spoken words into word-processed ones. You can then save the text in your favorite word-processing program, such as Microsoft Word.

What other tools do writers need? Paper, pens, paper clips, envelopes, of course (lots of them), a printer to work with your computer, a stand or desk for your computer or word processor, and a fax machine. All of these would be useful. This isn't everything that's needed, but it's a good start. It's also a great help to have an office, a room, or some place private to do your writing. Many writers use a specific room in their homes or apartments where they can be alone and turn out material without distraction or interruption.

A fancy office is not necessary. Neither is a slick executive desk or huge filing cabinets. Humans, especially those in creative fields, can adapt. Writers have written terrific articles on card tables, kitchen counters, dining room tables, porches, and on fast moving trains, jets, and slow buses.

Most writers do prefer one regular place to do their writing. Experiment to find out where you do your best work. Convert an extra room into a writing den. It need not cost much. Famous novelist John O'Hara (he also wrote his share of articles) wrote much of his first novel sitting on a bed in a hotel room.

Use your imagination regarding a place to do your writing. Some writers turn their garages into writing offices. Old farmhouses have been transformed into writing dens. Quite a few writers use a bedroom for a part-time writing study, or perhaps a spare attic or utility room. The main thing is to have a quiet place where you can work and where your computer, printer, paper, pens, and other items are always ready and waiting for your use.

There are other tools that are helpful in producing articles. The few listed here are for your future reference. They are not musts when beginning in article writing, but they will certainly be helpful to you, sooner or later.

- A quality dictionary. You have a variety to choose from, but a lot of writers like *Merriam-Webster's Collegiate Dictionary*.

- A filing cabinet, drawers, or some system for filing your material, correspondence, and articles in progress.

- Index cards. They are quite useful when doing research. Information can be written on the cards, with each new topic or fact given its own card. The cards can then be sequentially arranged, to help you structure your article.

- A tape recorder, microphone, and telephone recording adapter. They are helpful on interviews, provided the person being interviewed does not mind being recorded. (Some do mind, so you must give them a choice. It is also illegal in some states to tape record someone without permission. It's a good idea to state your intentions up front with whomever you are interviewing.)

- Letterhead. A professional looking letterhead is not a must, but it can help to create a favorable impression of you with editors.

- Writing tablets or legal pads. A number of writers use them for their longhand writing.

- An almanac. *The World Almanac* is very useful for general world facts.

- A good book of quotations.

- The annual edition of *Writer's Market*. It lists all kinds of article markets; payment rates; up-to-date names of editors; types of articles wanted; preferred article lengths; whether first, second, or all rights to the article are bought; and whether a given market pays on acceptance or publication.

- A thesaurus.

- Floppy disks, Zip cartridges, or Jazz cartridges for your computer.

- A monthly periodical on writing instruction and information. Both *Writer's Digest* and *The Writer* are quite good. Other new periodicals are available from time to time.

What Computer Systems and Software Are Right for You?

Personal computers have advanced dramatically since they were first introduced several years ago. Rarely do writers create anything on a typewriter anymore, for obvious reasons:

- To edit a typewritten page, you have to mark up your master document with an ink pen or cover up your mistakes with correction fluid. If an editor requests changes to your submission, the entire work must be retyped. It's a big hassle and the process can be slow.

- You can't use an automatic spell checker when you use a typewriter.

- Typewriters can disturb others—they're noisy.

- You can't e-mail a typed article to an editor working under a tight deadline; fax and mail are your only options.
- Using a typewriter is considered passé.

Computers, on the other hand, give writers much more flexibility. A PC is a writing, editing, and communication device all rolled into one. That's one of the reasons they are so popular—they empower writers in ways that are not possible without them.

What kind of computer system is right for you? It's really a question of taste. Most of today's major computers are very much alike. The difference between brands is almost nonexistent—Dell, Compaq, Hewlett-Packard, IBM, Gateway—they're all quality personal computer systems. Some people prefer the Macintosh instead—in fact, this book was put together on a Mac system. Whatever brand you ultimately choose, the final systems should be comprised of the following:

- *A mainframe computer system.* Most of the new models (even the basic systems) have plenty of speed and memory built in.
- *A monitor.* Either a 13- or 15-inch monitor will come standard. A 17-inch model, or greater, is recommended, however, if you can afford the extra cost.
- *A printer.* A good black and white laser printer (600 dpi) is recommended, although these days even a relatively inexpensive inkjet printer will provide clear copy and a wide range of type options.
- *A word processing program.* Microsoft Word, WordPerfect, and ClarisWorks are three popular programs.

That's all you need. Of course, if you want Internet access or games or any other special features, you will have to pay extra. But a basic computer system doesn't need to cost you a lot of money. One thing's for sure: You will realize many rewards by using a computer system in your day-to-day writing.

The Best Writing Routine for You

You will find the following practical pointers useful in getting more articles written and off to markets.

First, determine the best writing routine for you, including how much to write at a time and whether in longhand or directly on the computer. Most writers find it best to set a specific block of time to sit down and put words on paper. Once you decide on a time period, let nothing interfere with it.

You might choose one of the following time segments for your writing:

- 5:30 A.M. to 8:00 A.M. (good for part-time writers with a daily nine-to-five job)

- 9:00 A.M. to 1:00 P.M.

- 1:00 P.M. to 5:00 P.M.

- 7:30 P.M. to 11:30 P.M.

Some writers prefer the middle of the night. They find they can get a lot of work done from 11:30 P.M. to 3:30 A.M. or 2:00 A.M. to 6:00 A.M.

Here is a second practical pointer: If you find it hard to reserve a definite block of hours for writing, then try to determine the best time of day for you to write—early morning, afternoon, after dinner, or late at night. We suggest that you experiment by writing at different times of the day or night. In time, you'll discover what works best for you.

If a particular time of the day or night does not feel right for you, try a different time segment. Some writers are night people, others prefer the morning hours, and still others find the words flow best in the afternoon. You need to experiment till you find the ideal time slots for you. This is very important.

You may have noticed that the writing schedules mentioned here are rarely more than three to four hours. There is a good reason. After three to four hours, most writers have done their best for that day. To keep writing only means that the material has to be rewritten later. Give it your best shot for three to four hours straight each day. Then start fresh again the next day, or soon after. Naturally, there are some writers who can work for six to eight hours a day, but they are the rare and lucky ones.

The guidelines offered in this chapter encourage the valuable habits of a regular writing routine. Discipline is what really makes a writer. You can write successfully and profitably in time, providing you discipline yourself.

Writing Methods of Some Contemporary and Famous Writers

The methods of writing, the working hours, the place chosen for writing, and other factors naturally vary with the writer. Here are some of the working methods of some writers—both contemporary and of the past.

Victor Hugo: The immortal writer of *Les Miserables* followed an incredible schedule each day. He would be judged a chronic workaholic by today's standards. He was at his desk at 8:00 A.M. every morning and worked without rest till 2:00 P.M. He would start again at 4:00, stopping at 8 P.M. for a few hours of reading or relaxation. At 11:00 P.M., Hugo would put in some social time with friends. Finally, he would climb into bed at 1:00 A.M. or so in the morning. He needed only three to four hours of sleep each night before repeating his amazing schedule all over again.

Judith Krantz: As a successful article writer, before turning to novels, her advice is particularly worth noting: "Work regular hours, as if you were being monitored by a time clock. Have some sort of private place to work in, and learn to compose directly on a machine."

Ernest Hemingway: His target goal was between 450 and 575 words a day. To make up for an occasional lost day, he would write as much as 1,250 words. He preferred his ground floor bedroom as a workroom (in his Havana house), but he developed an early ability to work in almost any conditions.

Steve Allen: This prolific writer has turned out a lot of material over the years. Working at night is his preference. The interesting thing about Steve Allen is that he usually keeps multiple projects in progress at the same time. He may be working on articles, songs, and books simultaneously. If he gets bogged down on one type of writing, he switches to another.

James Michener: The late author wrote many articles, in addition to his fine novels and nonfiction. He did elaborate research and spent a great deal of time on his works. He stated that he thought he did some of his best writing "working in a cabin on Chesapeake Bay."

E. B. White: The author of many works, including the classic *Charolette's Web,* summed up his writing preparation with humor, saying, "Before I start to write, I always treat myself to a nice dry martini. Just one, to give me the courage to get started. After that, I am on my own."

The Master Key to Writing Success

There are three steps that can serve as a master key to your success in article writing. If followed consistently, these steps can help you to become an established writer.

1. Write every day (or at least five or six days a week).

2. Set a daily goal of a certain number of pages, or words, to be written. Then get them written no matter what.

3. Think regularly about the various markets to try and subject fields you might want to eventually specialize in (such as business, general interest, religious). In other words, plan ahead.

CHAPTER 5

Get It on Paper: Forty Ways to Get Started

This chapter is aimed at helping you see the many ways to create an article. Some stimulus, connection, or link in a writer's mind often leads to a new article. For example, you may feel lonely one rainy afternoon and, because of this feeling, decide to create an article about loneliness. Perhaps a glimpse of a dog watching over the street from a second-story window, prompts you to wonder what the animal is thinking, which leads to an article about animal intellect.

Ready for forty suggestions to whet your imagination? Here are some ideas to jump start your articles:

1. An interesting fact
Here is an example: *Yale Daily News* reported that 41 percent of Yale undergraduates (at this writing) are women. This interesting fact could lead to an article on the increased number of women at top colleges like Yale and Harvard.

2. An event
School, civic, musical, or sports events may all suggest a possible article. Example: You attend a play or a musical event at a local college or

community theater. Afterwards, you could write a review of the performance, or you might be inspired to research and write a piece about the playwright or composer.

3. A season of the year
One cold day in January, L. P. Wilbur began thinking about the miracle of spring and how it returns each year from March 21 to June 21. The result was a published article titled "The Return of Spring." The article brought several gratifying letters of praise from readers.

4. An observation
One day a grocer friend happened to remark that he "could count the number of his real friends on the fingers of one hand." This led to a published article on "The Miracle of Friendship." A statement by a companion or a bit of overheard conversation often provides inspiration.

5. A feeling, emotion, or mood
Your own feelings, or those shared by the public, can stimulate an article. One day L. P. Wilbur was watching his new car go through a supposedly reliable car wash. Three or four workers were inside on the back seat cleaning. Suddenly, they started joking with one another and jumping up and down in the car.

When the car was ready to go, L. P. discovered that both inside and outside mirrors had been tampered with, the tiltable steering wheel had been changed to a new position, and one of the floor mats was missing. Needless to say, the incident was extremely irritating.

Right on the spot, L.P. determined to write an article about today's modern car-wash businesses. No doubt many articles have been given life because a writer was shocked, angry, disgusted, or irritated about something.

6. Danger in everyday life
You could make a list of what is or may become dangerous in today's world. Some examples are: "Bankers Are Dangerous to Your Wealth," "Beware of the Little Green Monster," or "Drive Through That Town at Your Own Risk."

7. Visiting a place—even vicariously
"Vienna: Home of the Wiener," "The Place Where McDonald's Was Born," and "Nashville: A City for All Seasons" are a few examples.

8. A holiday
One way is to consider how various holidays affect people. How do prisoners feel on major holidays? What about poor people, those in hospitals, or those who live alone? Example: "Holidays Can Be the Loneliest Time of the Year."

9. An intriguing question
Here is an example: "What Makes a Successful Diplomat?" Other possibilities are "Will Time Travel Be Possible One Day?" and "Are UFOs for Real?"

10. Advice someone offered, including your own
Perhaps you feel you have some wisdom that would benefit a wide audience. Example: You might like to create an article that would inspire readers and help them find their purpose in life.

11. A quotation
Quotes have triggered hundreds—probably thousands—of new articles over the years. Example: Oracle CEO Larry Ellison made the following remark: "Microsoft's future is based on the idea of Windows everywhere. We think that will never happen. We think it will be the Web everywhere." This seemed like a natural article to Jon Samsel.

A writer encounters an enormous number of quotations during a career. So be alert for quotes that may have the seed of an article. They are out there. Look between the words. Examine the quotations you like from all angles.

12. A newspaper obituary
For example, "Dr. Joseph B. Rhine, who coined the term 'extrasensory perception' (ESP), died at age 84 today. Rhine and his wife were researchers for Duke University."

Here is another example: One day a headline in the evening newspaper read, "Actor Peter Sellers died early today without regaining consciousness after a heart attack. He was 54."

The obituary could just as well be about the late Frank Sinatra, Jimmy Stewart, Shari Lewis, Robert Mitchum, or any well-known person. Their passing triggers the article idea because readers always like summary-type articles about a star's life, a kind of memorial- or tribute-type article. Don't overlook reading the obits.

13. Statistical information

Shocking, alarming, or surprising numerical reports or statements may well suggest an article. Example: At this writing, some 65 million Americans are in debt to their maxed-out credit cards. This could be the seed for a number of articles about staying out of debt or not using or limiting the use of credit cards.

14. A belief held by many people

A spiritual, cultural, or religious belief can provide the springboard for a fascinating article. For example, reincarnation is a belief held by millions of people all over the world. Some reports have stated that half of all Americans believe in it.

After hearing a series of lectures on reincarnation a few years ago, L. P. Wilbur became fascinated by the topic, researched it, and eventually wrote a major article on the subject. Since then, some dozen or more articles about reincarnation have been published by L.P. in magazines and newspapers. Two possible titles for such an article on reincarnation might be "Do We Live Again?" or "If Reincarnation Is True, There's No Escape."

15. A wish to influence a certain business segment or career group

In the course of your work life, you may have gained experience or insight that could be valuable to professionals in other fields. To capitalize on this information, first choose the business or career group to whom you wish to direct your article—such as managers or supervisors—then create your article. Some examples are: "What It Means to Manage Others," "The Integrity of Today's Supervisor," and "What Is Executive Leadership?"

16. A particular type of problem: business, family, or personal

If you've encountered a problem, doubtless others have encountered it as well. Some examples: "The Naked Horror of Loneliness" and "The Problem of Too Little Sleep."

17. A declarative statement

Declarative statements are everywhere—from the printing on your breakfast cereal box to the business report, cookbook, tax form, or evening paper you read. Some declarative statements that have been the basis for articles include the following: "The world gets smaller every day" and "Good manners have gone out of style."

18. Received wisdom

There are many statements that have been made so often that we no longer question them, or even really think about what they mean. Writers can refresh these platitudinous statements by reinvestigating them, looking at them from new angles. Example: Consider the often expressed idea that there will be much greater use of robots in the years ahead. This could well lead to an article exploring the myths and realities of robotic technology.

Here is another possible example: The idea that it pays for writers to be as businesslike as possible in their work. We've all heard the statement, but a little clearheaded and specific advice is always welcome. Such an article would be right on target for any and all trade publications for writers.

19. A trait or quality that most people share, or can identify with

Example: Millions of people were fans of Marilyn Monroe. A touching tribute was once published about her that discussed her childlike quality, which comes across on the screen. Members of the human family share this trait of being childlike. The tribute was called "The Child in All of Us." Many other articles could be written about the common attributes of the human family.

20. A dramatic, unusual, or surprising phrase

We urge you to keep a special notebook of shocking phrases; they can often lead to article ideas. Keep your ears tuned for anything unusual, fresh, or captivating.

For example, a veteran insurance agent claimed he got results selling insurance by asking prospective clients the following question: "Will your widow dress as well as your wife does?" This triggered an article that was published in a major insurance publication.

Two other published articles using this method are "The Fastest Feet in the West" and "Damn Isn't God's Last Name."

21. A physical or mental condition

A health problem that you or someone close to you has endured could be the springboard for an article. Stories that tell how someone else has coped with hardship or heartbreak can be very meaningful for readers experiencing similar problems. Such articles can be research driven, and provide readers with information about treatments and medicines, or they can be subjective and deeply personal.

In a recent issue, the *New York Times Magazine* published a moving piece by Patti Davis about her father's (former President Reagan's) struggle with Alzheimer's disease.

22. People from the past

Both the well- and the lesser-known people furnish a constant source of material for writers. The study of a historical figure provides information about the momentous events and everyday life of bygone eras, which can be fashioned into fascinating articles. The struggles and passions of these people are also inspirational. Two examples are: "The Staggering Achievements of Victor Hugo," and "The Legacy of a Mad Man" (about Vincent van Gogh).

23. Various statements of command

You see these commands daily on billboards and in magazines, greeting cards, newspapers, and many other places. The "you" (meaning whoever reads the command) is implied in each one. Examples of command statements: "Hang in there," "Keep your chin up," "Make someone happy," and "Have a great day."

L. P. Wilbur was once captivated by a command statement originated by Jim Corbett, the famed boxer who knocked out the champion (of that era) John L. Sullivan: "Fight one more round." The command statement kept coming back to mind, and L.P. soon created an article on the philosophy of not giving up. In this case, the statement became the actual title of the published article.

24. An amusing or amazing encounter

There is an old saying that "truth is stranger than fiction." Events that occur in real life are often weirder, funnier, and more incredible than the stuff of fantasy. In your journal or notebook you should keep track of the funny conversations you are involved in, and the astounding incidents you observe. These can be written up and stand alone as short articles. *Reader's Digest* has whole pages devoted to real-life anecdotes. The *New York Times* publishes "Metropolitan Diary," a collection of such short tales, once a week, and many other local and regional publications publish similar features.

25. How to do something

Without a doubt, there is something that you are very good at, some area in which you not only have expertise, but also have a method or an insight that you could pass along to others—in writing. An example: "How to Pack Your Sales Presentation with Power."

26. A title
You can easily prove this to yourself by glancing over titles of various published articles. Some may suggest variations for new articles. A title can lead a writer to spin off other possible titles and, eventually, new articles. For example, you come across an article entitled "How Washington Wastes Your Tax Money." This title might lead to articles on how people waste time, or how the natural resources of a nation are wasted.

27. A hobby
Your favorite past time could spark an article. If you are an amateur cook, crafter, or collector, you could write about the joys of these activities. Author Michael Reynard actually turned his hobby—collecting the canceled checks of famous people—into an entire, published book, *Money Secrets of the Rich and Famous.*

28. A personality or celebrity
Well-known personalities and celebrities are always of interest to readers. Examples: "Brad Pitt: Myth in the Making," "Elvis Presley Predicted He Would Die Young," "Heather Graham Boogies Her Way to Stardom."

29. A cliché or overused expression
Clichés should be avoided within the article itself, but they may hold the seeds of possible thoughts or phrases that could lead to a new article. Examples: "Life with all its sorrows is good." The new article spurred by this was "Life Is Still Incredibly Good."

30. The signs of the zodiac
If horoscopes interest you, the zodiac may provide you with many ideas for articles. You might investigate the accuracy of horoscope predictions, or the veracity of the personality profiles for various signs. Example: "My Sister, the Leo."

31. Patriotism
Thinking about patriotism, an individual's, a group's, or a nation's, can lead to a variety of articles. Example: "The Sleeping Soldier at Arlington."

32. Your curiosity

Everyone is curious about something. Be guided by your own curiosity, and you will surely find a topic or question that will whet your reader's appetite. Examples: "What Will Space Colonies Be Like?" and "Why Do Dogs Do That?"

33. The effects of change

One way to get started is to list the changes ahead in the next century, then think about the effects of those changes and what people can do to be ready for them. Examples: "The Vanishing Inventor," "Solving the Y2K Problem."

34. A special promise or appeal to the reader

Readers are always looking for articles that will lift their spirits and make them feel happier about themselves and their surroundings. Titles that hold out hope for self-improvement or that offer escape into the imagination can be quite tantalizing. Some examples: "Hollywood's Second Golden Era," and "A Slimmer You in Thirty Days."

35. A key contemporary person

A sports hero, politician, deal maker, software giant—there are plenty of examples of people who are of current interest in your daily newspaper and monthly magazines.

36. A dream or a nightmare

Keep a journal next to your bed and keep a record of your nighttime visions. A few of them might spark article ideas. Example: "Monsters in the Closet and Other Childhood Fears."

37. One of the major professions

The legal, medical, and clerical professions can be the source of many effective articles. You could spend a lifetime writing about the personal, moral, political, etc., aspects of these vocations. An example: "Do Doctors Have the Right to Play God?"

38. Common everyday objects

Each day, millions of people take for granted and rely on a vast number of work-a-day objects—cups of coffee, ATM cards, staplers, radios, pocket change, pockets, toothbrushes, zippers, Ziploc bags. Without this minutia of everyday life, Western civilization would be sorely inconvenienced, to say the least. Common objects can spark many types of writing projects, from technical and cultural explorations to personal reveries and revelations.

39. Current and historical events of national and international import
Again, one need look no further than the daily newspaper to find a topic in this area. And, once again, these high-profile topics lend themselves to many different angles or approaches—the political, the psychological, the psycho-sociological. Two examples: "Ireland: Prisoner of the Past," and "The Russian Mafia in America."

40. The characteristics of a geographic area
This is similar to that of creating an article based on a place, but with a larger area in mind. Examples: "The Charm of Living in Scotland" or "Cape Hatteras: Graveyard of the Atlantic." Consider or study various geographic areas. When you travel in a new place, think of possible articles at all times; they are all around you.

We encourage you to read over this chapter, from time to time. As a writing exercise, select one of the suggested topics above and write a practice article. The process of writing will surely trigger other new ideas for articles.

—=◆=—

How to Organize Your Article: The Five *W*s and Other Techniques

Whenever you are stumped as to how to start an article, you need only think of this magic phrase—the Five *W*s. Immediately your mind will think: *who, what, when, where,* and *why.*

Nobody has ever counted them, but thousands upon thousands of articles have been started and completed via the help of the five *W*s. Journalists live by them. Newspaper stories must get to the point fast and report the key facts, so the five *W*s are basic, fast, and effective. Let's take a look at each one.

Who?

Leave the who of your article out, and your article is dead in the water. Readers want to know who it's about, or who did what, or who said what, as well as who the article is aimed at. A great many articles obviously hit the "who" question fast.

Take the article "Money Making Entrepreneurs," for example. No doubt at all is left in the reader's mind as to the *who* of the article. It is clearly meant for business people who are willing to take chances:

Are you willing to take risks? If so, then you have the major character-
istics of an entrepreneur, and possibly a money-making one.

The opening of the article continues to define and explain what it
means to be an entrepreneur, making it even clearer that anyone who
has ever thought of launching his or her own business will find the
article stimulating and helpful:

> By its very nature, entrepreneurship means being willing to think, orig-
> inate, and then execute your objectives and conclusions. Risk is
> involved throughout the process.

In another published article, L.P. tried to make it very clear in the
opening paragraphs that the *who* of the article was the founder of the
Coca-Cola Company. Actually, there were three founder-leaders that
made up the *who* in this case:

> Countless millions the world over would never think of letting a day
> go by without a nice cold bottle, can or fountain drink of Coca-Cola.
>   Three founder-leaders were behind the launching, early growth,
> and development of the legendary soft drink: Dr. John S. Pemberton,
> Asa G. Candler, and Robert W. Woodruff.

What?

Remember the Bachrach and David song *What's It All About, Alfie?* That
same question is in the readers' minds; they want to know what your
subject and article are all about. Don't make them wait several pages
or halfway through the article before it's clear; tell them quickly in
the early paragraphs.

In the published article, "Coping With Customer Skepticism,"
notice how the very first sentence spotlights the "what's it all about"
question, making the subject clear to the reader:

> A problem that most sales professionals face continually with certain
> prospects, customers, and clients is that of skepticism. This problem is
> in effect a thief because it can rob your chances for many sales. By
> knowing how to handle it, you are certain to sell more in the years
> ahead.

Here is another example, from an article titled "How Do You Face Crucial Moments?" Again, the very first sentence reveals the *what* instantly, and then the second paragraph poses a question and proceeds to analyze the *what* more:

> What do you do when the unexpected strikes? Do you blow with the wind or stand firm?
>
> Ever watch a racing car come off the track in apparent sudden trouble? Up till then, the driver may have had the race in the bag.

In the third paragraph an effective analogy is made between the car and the *what* of the article:

> Isn't life a lot like a race track? As babies we're cared for much like a new racing car. We take to the track in our teens, and really begin to hit the laps on the "young adult stretch." Then, as mature adults, we become "freeway flyers." From the start, we never know when we'll have to face a crucial moment, or how we will react to it.

When?

The *when* is one of the information blocks that build the article. *When* something occurred is very important. A film provides a good example here: Remember Jane Seymour and Christopher Reeve in *Somewhere in Time?* The viewer needed to know how far back in time Richard Collier (Reeve) was trying to get to, which was made clear, early in the story—1912. By the same token, article readers want to know when an event took place, when someone's life changed, when the family moved, when so-and-so hit the lottery. It gives readers a temporal context. Let them in on the "when" question, and you will keep them reading.

Look at the following example from a published article on the life and times of Walt Disney:

> From the day he arrived in Hollywood in the early 1920s, Disney's career covered a forty-three year period. Disney could not have picked a better time to make his move. During these golden years, the motion picture grew into an established and widely popular American art form. Walt Disney did much to help it attain this growth.

Where?

Where is closely related to *when*. Readers also need to know where the monument stands, where a war's final battle took place, where an accident took lives, where the number one vacation spot is currently. Remember the novel and film *The Bridges of Madison County?* When you think about it, that title is the *where* being answered. The entire novel is centered in the "where" question.

Here is a "where" example from the article titled "57 Ways to Sell a Pickle:"

> Success was no quick arrival in the life of Henry John Heinz. He started a vegetable garden in the 1860s outside his family's home, in Sharpsburg, Pennsylvania, and showed a talent and sense of soil and seed, which led to a surplus.

Notice how the second sentence of the opening paragraph situates the budding pickle czar in the exact place and time (where and when) from which his career was launched.

Why?

Last but not least is the *why*. Why did the teenager leave town? Why has the weather gone berserk in recent months and years? Why are Labrador retrievers so much sweeter and friendlier than other dogs? There are hundreds of *why*'s waiting to be answered. Your reader wants to know the answers.

In the article "Atlantic Theater Company: Evolving Structure" the *why* is introduced in the opening paragraph:

> It is not unusual for a group of actors, who have worked together as students, to dream of forming a theater company. But how many of these dreams actually become realities, and how many of them still exist, over a decade after inception? The Atlantic Theater Company is one such organization. . . . While the present managing director does not deny that an early mentor relationship with well-known playwright David Mamet had something to do with the group's initial successes, she affirms that it is the company's ability to self-evaluate and restructure that has guaranteed its survival.

This article was published in the *Theatre Administrator's Newsletter*. Why is the article of interest to theater administrators (the audience it was written for)? Because it tells the story of a small but successful company. Why has the theater company survived against normal odds? Because it has a unique ability to study its own process and learn from its mistakes. This is laid out in the first paragraph, and the rest of the article goes on to support this assertion, giving examples of the company's working methods.

Never underestimate the power of the Five *W*s. Think about them. You can come up with hundreds of new article ideas by just thinking about the Five *W*s and asking the questions they suggest, and then answering them with articles. Respect the Five *W*s, be alert to them, follow where they lead you. Think of them as your personal guides to a never-ending treasure hunt.

The Outline: Is It Necessary?

Before starting the actual writing of your article, you should decide whether or not to do an outline. Some writers dislike outlines and feel they are too rigid; others would never think of trying to start an article without one. An outlines is a road map. It offers a plan—a way for your article to develop.

Here is an example of an outline for a review of a performance that took place at the Brooklyn Academy of Music in New York City. A famous silent film, *The Passion of Joan of Arc*, was shown, and was accompanied by a modern choral work by composer Richard Einhorn.

I. Introduction
    A. What the event is, where and when it took place
    B. Points to cover
        1. Explore the relationship between the film and the score
        2. Talk about the experience of being in the audience for the combined works
        3. Examine the layers of meaning that are added to a work of art by the passage of time
        4. Explore the religious and mystical meanings of the film and the score

II. History of the Film
    A. The making of the film
    B. Reaction at the time
    C. Subsequent history
III. History of the score
    A. Why Einhorn chose this project
IV. Exploration of the cinematography and editing employed in *Joan*
V.   Exploration of the structure and instrumentation of the score
VI. The power of the combined experience

Note that the outline concisely lists each of the major points that the writer wants to cover and provides a blueprint for the structure of the article. Your outline can be much more (or less) detailed than this one, but it should give you a clear picture of where to begin and how to proceed. However, you need not stick to an outline exactly. New ideas and better ways of organizing sections may well come to you as you write.

A number of magazine editors ask to see an outline on an article idea before giving a writer the go-ahead. Outlines help an editor to see where you are going with an idea, how the article will be developed, perhaps what sections or headings it will use, the lead or hook, and your "take" on the information. In these cases, sending a sound, polished outline if the editor requests it may land you the assignment, and that could mean more money for your finished article.

You should be aware of something basic here: A number of article markets offer more money to the writer if the article was assigned by the editor. If you send the article in cold, the magazine may pay less. This is why it is most crucial to study article markets as often as possible so you know the policy of the magazine and how they work with writers. All the information you need to know is usually given in *The Writer's Market* listing for each market.

There are a number of writers who don't bother to do an outline. They simply send in their articles or submit a query by fax, e-mail, phone, or snail mail. They prefer to put all their focus on the article instead of an outline. You will have to experiment to see which way you prefer to work. Perhaps you will try an outline for some ideas while other ideas will be so well organized in your mind that they do not require one. It is wise to complete one, though, so you have one on hand if an editor asks for it.

The Parsing Method

You've completed your prep work. You've gathered together your writing supplies. You've prepared your writing workspace. You've even thought of a great idea for a story. Now you face a big obstacle—you cannot fathom how you will ever be able to churn out the 1,500 or 3,000 words to complete your article. Fear not! Even experienced writers have a difficult time with the "word count" issue, now and again. The important thing to remember is, where there's a will, there's a way.

To overcome this writing obstacle, pretend that several editors have given you go-aheads on these article ideas:

- A 1,500-word article on "What's Happened to Honor in America?" This article would deal with the subject of cheating.

- A 1,000-word article on "Every Age Has Its Compensations." This article would treat the advantages of every age level.

- A 2,000-word article on "Does Background Music Really Help?" This article would concern the pros and cons of recorded background music in buildings, offices, plants, and businesses.

At first glance, each of these projects seems like a lot of work. Two of the projects call for short lengths, although articles of 1,000 and 1,500 words don't look very short to a newcomer. What you need to realize is that the parsing method changes the perspective on these assignments. The parsing method is a simple procedure of mentally breaking down the "big number" into small, bite-sized chunks. By applying the parsing method to your writing task, you can turn what formerly looked like a great deal of work into easily manageable projects. Here's an example of applying the parsing method to three different articles:

- The 1,500-word article on the stock market crisis becomes 200 words a day for seven and a half days, or 300 words a day for five days.

- The 1,000-word article on honeymoons from hell becomes 100 words a day for ten days, or 200 words a day for five days.

- The 2,000-word article on jazz legends becomes 300 words a day for not quite seven days, or 200 words a day for ten days.

With the parsing method, it's much easier to get a piece of writing done, whether it's 1,000, 2,000, or 5,000 words. This is a most power-ful aid for any type of writing you do. If you look at the total number of words you must write, it may overwhelm you. But if you have an idea of where you are going, it will be relatively easy to complete a short portion each day, with each 200-word segment building toward the article's conclusions.

Now this advice is not really a secret. Many writers discover it sooner or later, often through trial and error. But not many novices to writing are aware of how it can help them. By using this simple method, you should be able to advance as an article writer much more quickly.

CHAPTER 7

Titles Catch the Reader's Attention

Titles are the calling cards of your articles. They are most useful for catching the reader's attention. Learn to come up with fresh and appealing titles, and you'll give your writing much more chance of being successful and profitable.

Titles are Headlines

Think of titles as headlines for your articles. You would be surprised how many readers check over only the titles of the articles in a publication before deciding which ones to read. The authors of this book do it, and many in the publishing business do the same thing. It's only natural to want to read first those articles with the most interesting or promising titles.

Titles make people buy. Dynamic titles for articles captivate readers and can make them so eager to read a given article that they start the piece on the spot, even before they have paid for the magazine or newspaper. Many magazine buyers pull out their money to buy because of title interest alone. It may be something curious, compelling, or newsworthy indicated by the title. The better the title list, the bigger the magazine sales.

Editors will sometimes change a title because they want the strongest one possible. A title may change any number of times, right up to an article's publication deadline. But its very helpful to both the editorial process and the writer's self-marketing efforts, if the article hits the editor's desk with a catchy moniker already in place. So, strive to write a title that grabs the reader fast. It's hard to do this consistently, but it is well worth the effort. Over a period of time, training and experience can help you write titles that sell.

Examples of Strong Titles

Here's a list of some effective titles. Look them over and see if you think you could improve them. Place a check mark beside those you especially like, then ask yourself why they appeal to you.

"The Lure of Faraway Places"
"Christopher Reeve: Man of Steel"
"The Brave New Workplace"
"Buying and Selling a House: The New Rules of the Game"
"Frightening Things About Fat"
"How to Develop Your Psychic Power"
"Whatever Happened to the Movies?"
"Computers in 2010"
"The Things You Learn After You Know It All"
"How to Handle Blue Mondays"
"10 Secrets Wives Keep from Their Husbands"

Notice how many of the words employed in these titles act as hooks to capture the reader. Words like "lure," "new," "frightening," "psychic," and "secrets" all promise to reveal something unknown or unexpected to the prospective magazine buyer. The phrases themselves are short, informative, and authoritative. From these short headlines the reader can glean the author's take on the subject.

How to Create Fresh Titles

One of the best ways to come up with a strong, fresh title is to read the finished article several times. You can often derive a good title from the material itself.

- Stay alert at all times for snappy lines, short and to-the-point questions, expressions, and sentences that seem to sparkle and leap out at you. Any of these can spawn a good title.

- Practice examining the titles of already published articles to see how you might word them differently. Don't be afraid to borrow the idea behind a title and express it in your own words. A title cannot be copyrighted. You have free rein to experiment with those you come across for your own articles. It would not, however, be good practice to use exact titles already published. Editors might rightfully frown on this. Try instead to come up with your own original and strong titles.

- Look for key phrases in the article that seem to sum up what it's about. You will often see a key line or phrase that puts it all in a nutshell.

L. P. Wilbur once wrote an inspirational article on the deep meaning of Christmas. The challenge? How to treat the birth of Jesus of Nazareth in a fresh way. The answer? Comparing the D-day invasion to Jesus' invasion of Earth.

After much thought and a number of attempts at a beginning for the article, an effective analogy was achieved. The article began, "It was fifteen minutes past midnight. Not far from five beaches lay the greatest fleet of warships the world had ever known." The article went on to describe the courage, bravery, and fear of June 6, 1944 (D day), when the Allies invaded Normandy.

After finishing the introductory paragraph, L.P. wrote the following:

There was another day on which an invasion took place. There were no warships in this invasion, no guns, no thousands of men waiting to land on a beach. This invasion had a Supreme Commander too—a Supreme Commander of love. His invasion sign was a star of faith, hope, and redeeming love. The entire armada in this invasion was the birth of a child; a child named Jesus who became a man.

The entire 1,500-word article was complete, but L.P. could not think of a title. After reading the article numerous times and wracking his brain, L.P. suddenly realized that the strongest title was the simplest and most obvious one. The whole piece revolved around the comparison of Jesus' birth to the invasion of Normandy. Why not call the article "The Earth's D Day"?

Titles Lead to Articles

A lot of writers begin an article only when they have a strong title in mind. Here is an idea that often works well. When you don't have a specific title in mind, use a "dummy" title (a temporary one) while working on the piece. "The Incredible Versatility of Thomas Jefferson" was a substitute title used for a work-in-progress article on the former president of the United States. This isn't a bad title, but it certainly does not leap off the page. A better title is "The Genius of Jefferson." It's better because it's shorter and more to the point. All the ways in which Jefferson was versatile added up to one key word: "genius." "The Genius of Jefferson" appeared on the final published article. Sometimes having a working title that you can mull over can lead to a better one.

If you can come up with new titles on a regular basis, you may be able to increase your profit margin. How can you do this? One way is by reading your old articles from time to time (yes, those you have not sold yet) and giving them fresh, original titles. Professional writers do this all the time. If an article won't sell under one title, another one may be just what is needed to make it click with the next editor. We've know numerous writers who sold an article on the tenth, twentieth, or thirtieth submission to a market. It took L.P. forty-nine attempts to sell one article. Why did it sell on the forty-ninth time at bat? Because it was given a new, more interesting title. No other changes were made.

Titles Are Fun to Write

Since a title often sums up the entire idea and scope of an article, there is a continuous challenge to come up with quality ones. Many writers find this name game most interesting.

You may find in time that you have become a title collector. No matter where you go or what you do, your mind will be alert to any and all possible title ideas for future articles. Many will be useless to you, but you're certain to come up with a number of gems, if you keep at it long enough. Some writers have been collecting titles for decades.

Another way to stay alert for titles is to review the following list of the various kinds available. You might call it your title potential:

- Surprise titles
- Shock titles
- Question titles
- Command titles
- Punch line titles
- Statement titles
- Dramatic titles
- Geographic titles
- Trick titles
- Catchphrase titles
- Musical titles
- Short titles
- Long titles
- Alliterative titles (using words beginning with the same consonant sound)
- VIP name titles (the name appears in the title)
- Sad titles
- Happy titles
- Military titles

Key Points to Remember

- Titles are the labels, headlines, or calling cards of your articles.
- Key phrases, snappy lines, pointed questions, and other ideas in your articles can lead to an effective title.
- A title cannot be copyrighted. Titles of existing articles can be paraphrased, updated, and otherwise changed into new titles.
- Magazine buyers often read the list of article titles before deciding whether to buy.
- A good title can suggest itself after the article has already been finished.

- It's a good idea to come up with several titles for an article and choose the strongest.
- Writing fresh titles for old articles (those you have not sold yet) can increase your sales and profits.

Practice Exercises

1. Write an interest-grabbing title for an article on pro wrestling.

2. Which of the following two titles do you like best, and why? "The 10 Most Common Barriers to a Successful Marriage" "Success Secrets of Happily Married Couples"

3. Do you think the title "Feelings" is too short? Why or why not?

4. Find a published article and write a new title for it. Is your new title better than the published one? How?

5. Imagine the opening sentence for an article titled, "Road Rage: Barbarians on the Highway."

CHAPTER 8

The Lead Is Critical

Can a fisherman expect to catch anything without bait? That would be a bit like trying to get a plane in the air with no wings. By the same token, the opening of an article, which is called the lead, is the bait used to hook readers—and editors—and whet their appetite for your article. Never underestimate the great importance of the lead.

The lead grabs the reader's attention and makes him keep on reading. Many think the lead (opening) paragraph should contain all five Ws discussed in chapter 6: who, what, when, where, and why.

Types of Leads

By studying the different styles of leads, you will find writing the opening to be less confusing. Here are some of the many types of leads:

- *Human interest.* L. P. Wilbur once did an article on Ira Hayes, the young marine who became a national hero for his part in the flag raising on Iwo Jima in World War II. The lead just wouldn't click; after several unsuccessful attempts, L. P. simply stepped back and let the research simmer in his mind a little longer.

A few days later, he was able to write the following lead, which was the opening of the published article: "That well-known picture of a marine squad and a sailor raising the American flag at Iwo Jima has a unique story behind it."

It was a good lead because the picture is one of the most memorable and representative of all war photographs. It is well known and evocative of courage, endurance, and determination for many Americans.

- *Question.* This kind of opening reveals the entire scope of the article. The rest of the article proceeds to answer the question "Ever spend an entire cold day hunting a deer, only to find that your family would not touch the meat when you got it home and cooked it?"

  Notice how the writer puts the reader into the scene through the use of the word "you." The author isn't talking about any old hunter whose family will not eat the meat on the table; the reader *is* the hunter and it is the *reader's* family who is ungrateful for the bounty provided. Therefore the reader is automatically very involved in the situation, and will keep on reading to find out how the writer answers the question and resolves the problem.

- *Dramatic lead.* Many articles dealing with dangerous vocations, hobbies, or personal experiences use this attention-getting lead. All forms of the dramatic may be used for such leads. "The single-engine plane climbed to 5,300 feet. Dick Mason dropped from the fuselage and began to plummet toward the earth at a free-fall speed of 126 miles per hour."

  The cliff-hanger ending of the lead sentence compels the reader to keep on reading.

- *Flashback.* "Humans have been changing their environment (and adapting to it) since their first dim days on earth when the sun was their sole source of heat." This lead reminds the reader that whatever happens today is part of the continuum of history.

- *Statistical lead.* Open with numerical facts related to the subject. "According to the National Eye Institute in Bethesda, Maryland, approximately 10 million Americans over the age of sixty have visual impairments." A statistical quote from a reputable source can establish the writer's credibility. Of course, statistics can also be used to amaze and shock readers.

- *Location.* This opening names and describes a specific place or area. "Wall Street is a narrow street four blocks long in lower Manhattan." This lead infects the reader with a sense of anticipation. What interesting facts is the author going to reveal about this insignificant scrap of real estate, the reader wonders?

- *Dialogue.* "John, I know you can do better in school." "Dad, it's my teacher. She doesn't explain it in a way that I can understand." In this lead, several characters are introduced who can be developed and referred to throughout the article.

- *Scene description.* "Mrs. Brown is doing her weekly food shopping and has just selected a supply of her family's favorite breakfast cereal: a popular brand of corn flakes." The reader is in the supermarket observing Mrs. Brown. This kind of lead can be effective because it engages the reader in the action of the story.

- *Definition or informational lead.* "Gout is a type of arthritis. It consists of 'drops' of uric acid that accumulate in the soft tissues of the body. In fact, the word gout is from the Latin word *gutta,* meaning drop." An opening that reveals the author's knowledge of the facts establishes his credibility and gains the reader's trust.

- *Philosophical statement.* "Success is doing the most that is humanly possible with all that you've got." This upbeat, encouraging statement extends a friendly invitation to the reader.

- *The command.* "Your sales force is selling quality RVs, but they are also selling the idea of travel and all that goes with it. Get more sales this month, and in the ones to follow. Sell prospects the luxury of RV travel." A lead like this one promises an inspiring and instructive article will follow.

The leads described are not the only ones, but they are some of the most widely used. Here are other types of article leads you can choose from:

- The shocking lead
- The humorous lead
- The comparison or contrast lead
- The verse or poem lead (open with a suitable poem)
- The quotation lead (open with an apropos quote from a well-known person)

How to Write Better Opening Paragraphs

When the eyes of an editor or a million or more readers fall on the opening paragraph of your article, it had better have enough appeal to keep them reading. The opening puts your article center stage; it announces what you have to report, expose, describe, or amuse. You want your opening to do you proud, to hit the reader right between the eyes and flash the command message, "You must read this article!"

A good lead paragraph gets to the point fast; sets the stage for the article; is preferably on the short side; and packs in key facts that add incentive for the reader to keep reading. The lead paragraph should arouse interest or curiosity in the reader and provide an overview of what is to follow. In some cases, making frequent use of the word "you" is helpful because the most interesting person in the world— from the reader's point of view—is the reader. The "you" lead actually puts the reader in the article. The names of famous people or celebrities in the lead sentence or paragraph can increase the magnetic power of the opening. A witty or clever opening often works well. It provokes interest and makes a reader want more. Sometimes exaggeration can be useful, providing you do not distort the factual information of your article. Up-to-the-minute data can provide a strong lead for a news story.

Remember, anything and everything you can use to get the reader involved in your article is fair game. As with all other aspects of writing, your ability to write leads and openings will improve with practice. Hone your skill at writing crisp, dynamic leads, and you will begin to see a real difference in your work.

Take a look at the following effective article openings:

> Back when I had nature study in school, a nature lover was somebody who liked to look at sunsets and waterfalls and maybe take a few snapshots. We knew nature included bugs and weeds, too, but you didn't have to like them. Times change. [The article goes on to say why the cutest animals are so often the most troublesome.]
>
> —"Of Mice and Me" (*McCalls* magazine)

The writer of this article uses a flashback lead, referring back to when "nature" was a subject studied in school. A definition of a nature lover is given, and then quickly contradicted by the statement "times change." This opening sets the stage for an article about nature, written from a perspective that is clearly somewhat wary of the more earthy parts of the natural world. It piques the reader's curiosity and promises to be amusing.

> Look at almost any successful person, and you'll find that confidence is usually part of the reason for his or her success.
> —"Confidence in Yourself Is Money in the Bank"
> (The *American Salesman*)

This opening lures the reader via the promise of teaching more about the value of confidence in sales and marketing. The first sentence is to the point, giving a basic reason why the article should be read.

> Making a sale is only one step in the process for savvy independent agents. Instead of viewing the closed sale as the end of the process, look at it as the resource for a network of new sales—by referred leads. To skip this step is like throwing away money you find in your pocket.
> —"The Referred Method" (*Professional Agent*)

Many strong openings grab the reader with a short, on-target sentence. This article is a good example. The lead sentence arouses curiosity, plus a desire to read more. Many sales people do think the selling process is over once the sale is made, but this article's opening reveals that a case is going to be made for the importance of obtaining referred leads from the brand new customer or client. The opening also ends with a warning to the reader, which makes it seem more urgent that the reader continue studying the article.

> Should you or should you not? Keep a diary, that is. I don't mean a personal diary, though you may already have one going. What about starting and maintaining a supervision diary? Why not? Let's look at the pros and cons of the idea. Then you can make your own decision.
> —"Pros and Cons of Keeping a Supervision Diary"
> (*Supervision Magazine*)

The article uses a "Hamlet"-type opening with a pointed question. Sometimes a question will work well as your very first sentence. The next few sentences clarify what the question involves. Again, this type of opening can stimulate reader curiosity.

I was fired for loving America. It sounds crazy, but that's what happened. I was fired because I put an American flag decal on my hard hat
in support of our country.
    —"America Means More to Me Than My Job" (*National Enquirer*)

This opening provides a strong example of a startling statement.
The very first sentence hooks the reader and makes him or her wonder how such a thing could happen. The next few sentences reveal
the reason for the firing, and underline the patriotism of the writer.

When other techniques don't seem to work, keep the startling
statement in mind. Many a reader would feel compelled to read this
article after such a surprising opening.

We mutually pledge to each other our lives, our fortunes and our
sacred honor.   —"A Question of Honor" (*Reader's Digest*)

In this lead the writer uses a famous quotation to grab the reader's
attention. Honor and patriotism have strong appeal and get the reader
into the article fast. Passionate and interesting quotes can often be an
excellent way to open an article.

How do your attitudes toward competition affect your opportunity for
advancement? How do your feelings about your competitors affect the
success of your business? More than you might realize.
    —"Sharpen Your Competitive Edge" (*Her Street Journal*)

Again, the question opening is a popular one, and this article
poses a query that many business owners may not have asked themselves recently: Just how does a person's reaction to competition, and
his or her feelings about competitors, affect the prosperity of a business? Note that this article ran in a journal that is published for
businesswomen, so these questions would be particularly significant
to the target audience. The lead pulls the reader into the article by
bringing up matters that directly concern the owner of any business.

The world of self-employment is wide open and offers you a variety of
opportunities. A few of the many possibilities include mail-order typing, résumé, or other services you can provide, and virtually any kind
of business you offer for a fair price. You really have quite a choice.
    —"The Self-Employment Picture" (The *Elks Magazine*)

Here, self-employment is spotlighted as an alluring and available opportunity.

Remember these guidelines that will help you to write better openings:

- Keep your opening on the short side (the beginning paragraph or two).
- Don't neglect the "you" lead; it actually puts the reader in the article.
- The names of famous people or celebrities in the opening can be powerful hooks.
- A witty or clever opening often works well. It makes the writer's voice attractive and accessible, and makes the reader want more.
- Exaggeration can be useful. Watch the professional comedians to see how they make effective use of this tool.
- Ultra-current facts and plenty of action make strong leads for news stories.
- Practice writing crisp, dynamic openings; this is the ideal way to gain skill in constructing leads.

What to Do When Nothing Works

There will be times in your article writing when you can't seem to come up with the right opening for a particular piece. After trying all the options with no positive results, there's another solution available to you: a change of scenery.

Some articles are tougher to write than others are. Sometimes you just aren't all that interested in the subject. Go for a walk; visit a local art gallery. A change of location and scenery at such times will often get the creative juices flowing again when you get home. Or, you might want to take your notepad or laptop with you to the reading room at the library, or a picnic table in the park. You may find that tough lead much easier to write while in a fresh setting.

Practice Exercises

1. What would be your lead for an article entitled, "Is the Presidency Too Big for One Person?"

2. Choose any published article you really like. Write a new opening for it. Then compare your own opening with the published one. How did your approach differ from the author's?

3. Assume you are writing an article on the things you like best about the region, city, or town where you live. Write three leads for the article, then choose the one you like best. Analyze why you chose that particular opening.

4. Read five published articles of your choice. Study the type of lead used in each.

CHAPTER 9

———⋙⋆⋘———

An Article Is a Series of Paragraphs

Ah, the paragraph—that's what brings articles to life. Paragraphs are the building blocks of articles. Create well-written paragraphs and that will usually lead to a well-written article. Without paragraphs, an article is dead in the water.

Each time you start a new article, realize that it's the combined paragraphs that comprise the piece. If you think too much about the article as a whole (or the total amount of work necessary to complete it), it may put you off. Try to keep in mind that enough well-ordered paragraphs will eventually bring you to a logical ending. A great many articles will almost write themselves if the writer focuses on one paragraph at a time. Create a solid paragraph to follow the lead and you're usually on your way.

The Paragraph: Content and Structure

Imagine how crude and illogical it would be if an article had no paragraphs at all from beginning to end. Wouldn't it be difficult to read one long block of words? You bet it would.

Paragraphs are like a string of pearls. The string is the subject or theme being highlighted or presented. The paragraphs are the pearls whose combination produces the finished article with its resulting impact and effect.

What is an effective paragraph? At first glance, a paragraph does seem to be merely a number of sentences strung together. On a deeper level, a paragraph consists of a deliberate series of well-phrased sentences. Northwestern University professor John H. Barber, Ph.D. says "effective writing is a language-based interaction between writer and reader that promotes a sense of 'reality,' believableness, or involvement." Obviously, the way to build good, solid paragraphs is to start with effective sentences that follow this guideline.

Most paragraphs are structured using these guidelines:

- A strong opening sentence makes clear what the paragraph will be about. The first paragraph sets the stage and seeks to interest the reader.

- The paragraph's midsection supports the opening statement.

- The last lines of a paragraph wraps up all loose ends and ends the thought process with a satisfactory conclusion.

Four Sample Paragraphs

Ken Orton didn't set out to revolutionize the e-commerce travel market. In fact, what he initially set out to do was transform a TV-based travel programming company into a networked online travel business. What Orton and team managed to do in the process is shake up the $101 billion U.S. travel agency market—growing their company, Preview Travel, into one of the most comprehensive, easy-to-use, and enjoyable travel destinations on the Internet.

The author starts by piquing the readers' interest. He states that Ken Orton didn't intend to change the face of the travel market, but implies, with this statement, that Mr. Orton somehow, in spite of himself, set this revolution in motion. The reader is engaged and wants to find out exactly what it was that Mr. Orton *did* intend. The author fulfills the readers' expectation by supplying this information, and then goes on to relate exactly what Mr. Orton achieved. This is a successful paragraph because it grabs the reader's interest and sets out the content and direction of the rest of the article.

High school days are wonderful times, but they go by faster than most people realize. If you haven't already done so, now is the time to be zeroing in on what you honestly feel is the right vocation for you.

In this article, clearly aimed at adolescents, the author again arrests the reader's attention with the first sentence—this time through the use of contrast. Yes, the writer agrees, in the first half of the sentence, it is wonderful to be young, but he quickly pulls the rug out from under his readers by flatly stating that it won't last for long. He follows this sobering remark with a sentence that announces the topic the article will cover: choosing a vocation.

Bill Gates has never been accused of missing an opportunity to make a buck. So a lot of people got excited when Gates launched his Microsoft Network, dedicated to harnessing the Internet's awesome potential for delivering product to bring entertainment in myriad, interactive forms to a computer screen near you. Didn't work out. MSN is already a distant memory in the nanosecond attention span of the digital world. Bill's folded his tent and gone home. A lot of investors who have tried to profit from Web-based entertainment were not surprised that the effort failed, though most everyone was unnerved at how quickly Gates decided to jump ship on the effort.

This paragraph, from an article about Web-TV, also makes use of contrast, as well as metaphor. The roller coaster of Microsoft Network's history is presented, cleverly and succinctly, as if Internet-based entertainment were an unclaimed wilderness, and Mr. Gates a potential conqueror. In the beginning, Microsoft sallies forth with a flourish to "harness the Internet's awesome potential" and, just two sentences later, Bill folds his tent and goes home.

We've all heard that ageless expression: "Practice makes perfect." But does it really? If so, why do some drummers practice almost endlessly, only to achieve limited results, while others practice a minimum amount of time and advance rapidly?

In chapter 5 we suggested that an overused expression could provide the stimulus for an article. The paragraph above opens with a cliché, but only for the purpose of investigating its truth. The next two sentences challenge the "ageless expression." The paragraphs that follow answer the questions that this paragraph has raised.

Like a String of Pearls, Paragraphs Linked Together Build Articles

Now that you have a sense of what a single paragraph encompasses, let's look at how these entities build, one upon the other, to form a completed article.

- The first paragraph sets the stage and seeks to interest the reader.

- The second paragraph often expands the first, clarifies the direction, or makes clear the intent or purpose of the article. A good second paragraph should get the reader to want to read on, tell why the reader will benefit from the article, offer a preview of what is to come, or establish a mood for the material.

- Each additional paragraph builds on the previous one until the introduction to the article has been established. Some articles' beginning sections use only one or two paragraphs. Others take several paragraphs to set the beginning.

- Once the scope and direction of the article have been introduced, the paragraphs continue to build on each other to form the middle of the article. For more information about how to construct the body of an article, see chapter 10, "How to Create a Midsection That Doesn't Sag."

- The closing paragraphs of an article often repeat the key points made.

Even if you have never written an article before, here are two important points to keep in mind. First, once you learn how to write a clear, simple sentence—and this comes with experience—you can certainly write a paragraph; second, if you can write a paragraph, you can definitely complete articles of all kinds and sell them for money.

Building paragraphs into a solid article can be fun, once you understand the process and gain some confidence. Keep the following pointers in mind when you construct your paragraphs:

- See how many different ways you can construct a paragraph. It's entirely possible to plan or outline a paragraph. Decide what you want each sentence in a paragraph to accomplish.

- When one or more paragraphs do not measure up, start over again.

- View the completion of each paragraph as a challenge to your writing ability.

Transitions Between Paragraphs

Transitions are bridges that move the reader out of one paragraph into another. The better your transitions, the smoother your article will read.

Here are some popular kinds of transitions:

- Start a new paragraph with a quotation.

- End the old paragraph with a question, and start the new paragraph with an answer; or begin the new paragraph with a question and answer the question within that same paragraph. As each paragraph takes up a new thought or related aspect of the subject, a question is often a good way to move into a fresh paragraph. A word of caution. Don't overdo the question-and-answer technique; it could begin to sound singsongy and irritatingly repetitive.

- Find a phrase or word at the end of the last paragraph you have written and repeat or echo it. This often makes for a smooth transition.

Examples of Paragraph Transitions

In an article titled, "New Success Secrets," which was to be published in *Salesman's Opportunity* magazine, L. P. Wilbur needed to show the reader how to strengthen his or her selling personality in order to become more successful. Here is an example of the transition used:

> Secrets for more success are actually tied in with your personality. By improving your weak personality factors and putting more firepower behind your strong qualities, your selling personality can continually grow into a dynamic and powerfully attractive force.

Next came the transition sentence leading into the third paragraph of the article: "Think of your selling personality as a magnet."

The first paragraph suggests that the personality can be powerful and attractive. The first sentence of the next paragraph takes that concept and turns it into a metaphor (the magnet), which the reader can use as a mental image in order to improve his or her selling power.

In an article titled, "The Self-Employment Picture" (published in The *Elks Magazine*), notice the transition between the first and second paragraphs:

> The world of self-employment is wide open and offers you a variety of opportunities. A few of the many possibilities include a résumé service, house cleaning, investment information, and virtually any kind of business you offer for a fair price. You really have quite a choice.
>
> The Small Business Administration says that there is one chance in five that a new business will still be operating and actually run by the same owner after a 10-year period.

Again, contrast is employed, this time in order to string together two paragraphs. The first presents self-employment as an area rich with golden opportunities, while the second cautions that the odds against business survival are high. The statistics are taken from and attributed to a highly credible source, the Small Business Administration.

Heavy-Duty and Easygoing Paragraphs

We urge you to launch an ongoing study and critical analysis of articles. In your study, you will notice that some articles have mostly hardworking paragraphs. By this we mean that the paragraph is dense with information and ideas, and thus "working hard" to impart data or concepts to the reader. Usually, this means that the reader, too, will have to work hard, reading the paragraphs with extra concentration. Other articles have lighter, easygoing paragraphs.

It's certainly possible for you to plan the paragraphs of each article you write. Many writers do this in advance. You should try this method and see how it works for you.

Here are some specific guidelines to plan the paragraphs of an article:

- Use phrases separated by dashes to describe the contents of each paragraph.

- Write a simple statement of what you want to say or accomplish in each paragraph of your article.

- Use the list method, similar to the following example, taken from Jon Samsel's article entitled "The 'Groundhog Day' Phenomenon: A Lesson in Customer Convenience":

Paragraph 1—Present question: Why don't online companies offer better customer support?

Paragraph 2—Explain the change in the market that is responsible for this phenomenon.

Paragraph 3—Explain the advantage (convenience) of online transactions.

Paragraph 4—Describe the film *Groundhog Day*.

Paragraph 5—Explain the connection between the film and subject of this article

If you want to see how this paragraph "outline" plays out in the finished article, you will find it reproduced in full, in appendix B.

Always be aware that one paragraph may communicate a number of key facts and information, while another may simply give the reader time to digest what has just been said or to summarize. Avoid too many long, complicated paragraphs in a row. These may tire the reader. Use an occasional catch-up paragraph or time-to-digest paragraph if your article deals with an involved or technically complex subject.

If an article has nothing but long paragraphs full of information, figures, and hard-to-follow, complicated material, you run the risk of losing the reader's attention. By the same token, if your article consists of only light, easygoing paragraphs, you may also lose the reader. Much, of course, depends on the nature of the article subject, the way you handle it, and the type of person reading the article. Many readers and publications want only light material, while others look for more in-depth discussion and analysis.

Pay attention to how other writers combine heavy and light paragraphs.

Points to Remember

- An article is a series of paragraphs.
- A paragraph can be planned or outlined in advance.
- Paragraph transitions are bridges that ease the reader out of one paragraph and into the next.
- Some popular transitions use a question, a quotation, or repeat a word or phrase from the end of the previous paragraph.

Practice Exercises

1. Write a short paragraph on your favorite subject, then rewrite to improve it. Read over your first effort and then your improved one.

2. Write a solid paragraph on "A Paragraph Is Like a String of Pearls."

3. Write an opening paragraph for an article titled "Where Do You Expect to Be in Five Years?" Decide if you like what you have written. Ask yourself how it could be made more interesting and readable.

4. Write three opening sentences for each of the following titles: "The Teacher I Remember Most and Why" and "There's a Child in All of Us." Decide which one you like better and why.

5. Begin two short articles on subjects of your choice. Alternate from one to the other, writing a new paragraph for each article. This will prove to you that you can have two articles in the works at the same time. When you get bogged down in one—or just tired of working on it—switch to the other one.

CHAPTER 10

How to Create a Midsection That Doesn't Sag

In the memorable words of an article expert, "A good magazine article today must have a solid framework. It must have a theme, make a point of some kind, and drive toward a conclusion." Our thanks to Max Gunther, a long respected dean of article writing, for this definition.

The objective of the middle of your article is to expand on the subject, develop it, and discuss the major points. You must persuade, convince, entertain, inspire, or otherwise accomplish the purpose of your material. You can quickly see the importance of a well-planned and informative midsection.

How is the excellence you want achieved? The secret to good article writing is to make effective use of the typical elements of most midsections. Here we will take each of the elements of a midsection and focus on the contribution it makes to the total article.

Elements of a Midsection

These magic ingredients do a great deal to bring an article to life, give it substance and depth, and hold the reader's interest. The body of an article is often formed by using the following key elements:

- Anecdotes
- Examples
- Statistics
- Quotations
- Sample reports
- Comparison or contrast
- Illustrations and sidebars (pictures)

Anecdotes

The *American College Dictionary* describes an anecdote as "a short narrative of a particular incident or occurrence of an interesting nature." For an article writer, an anecdote is a very short story with a point. The best anecdotes have a beginning, middle, and end. Little stories like this help illustrate the basic point or purpose of an article. In fact, if you have a gift for storytelling, you already have an important tool for writing articles.

Here is an example of an anecdote:

Not long ago, a young man and his wife from Memphis were killed in an auto accident. This young man—only twenty-seven—was just beginning his life's work, although he had already revealed much promise. "Equal Justice Under the Law," an essay he had written while he was still a teenager, had won top prize in a writing contest.

This anecdote was part of an article about the words that are remembered after people die. It was included to illustrate the fact that people can leave a living legacy of noble thoughts and moving sentiments, even if they are cut off in the prime of life. Stories like this evoke an emotional response in the reader, and can be a powerful way to keep him or her connected to your article.

The reading public is very interested in anecdotes about celebrities because these little stories humanize well-known people, and make their personalities and their actions understandable. This anecdote from an article about General George Patton shows that his character was firmly established in his youth:

General George Patton's fighting spirit revealed itself clearly at West Point. While many of his fellow students disobeyed the academy's rules, Patton was serious about them and believed in keeping them.

One day the future general saw a classmate breaking a rule and felt he had to report it—a rule required by the West Point code. Later that night, several of the largest and toughest cadets visited George and threatened him with a beating should he make the report and squeal. Patton calmly replied, "I'm reporting him. I'll fight you now, one at a time, and when I get out of the hospital I'll start again where I left off." Nobody accepted his offer.

Readers are human and enjoy little stories that illustrate a point, illuminate a truth, or help them visualize an event. Anecdotes are very useful to a writer because of their power. In fact, a number of working writers collect or save them for future use in articles. Remember, articles you write will be much more interesting, and will engage the reader's emotions, if you make use of appropriate anecdotes.

Where to Find Anecdotes

If you're serious about article writing, the authors strongly urge you to start saving anecdotes for future use in the articles you will write. You will be giving yourself a big head start toward more sales. Here are some useful anecdote sources you can start tapping at once:

- *Your own past.* Search your memory. You are bound to discover a rich variety of little stories you can use from your youth, school days, jobs you have held, hobbies, or travel.

- *Incidents in the media.* You can put stories from magazines, newspapers, newsletters, or bulletins into your own words or use them as they are, if they are not too long (and you cite the source).

- *Your friends, neighbors, and relatives.* This can be another rich source. When you hear a good anecdote related by a friend or relative, get it down on paper fast while it's fresh in your mind.

- *Books.* They are a fertile source for anecdote material. There are even whole books devoted to the subject of anecdotes!

As time passes, you will eventually develop quite a backlog of anecdotes. Once you have a lot of them, you might wish to divide them into categories. Then, when you are writing various articles, you have only to thumb through your anecdote file cards to select those you want to use. This system may not work for every writer, but the authors can vouch for the help it has provided them.

Here is a suggested anecdote category list:

- Humorous anecdotes
- Anecdotes about money and personal finance
- Health and job anecdotes
- School and college anecdotes
- Anecdotes from the military
- Travel anecdotes (this can be a very rich source)
- Anecdotes about marriage

Basic Tips for Using Anecdotes

Here are some basic guidelines for using anecdotes in the articles you write:

1. Anecdotes may be used anywhere in an article. They usually appear in the body, but many articles open with an interest-grabbing anecdote. For example, *Reader's Digest* likes opening anecdotes.

2. Even seemingly unimportant incidents can be used as anec-dotes. Don't rule out trivial-sounding events—the morning you got caught in the rain, the time the telephone repair per-son was exceedingly courteous, etc.

3. Anecdotes can vary in length—from a few lines to several paragraphs—but they are usually short.

Remember also that anecdotes can be repeated in different arti-cles. L. P. Wilbur has used the following story several times in differ-ent contexts to make the point that glory and fame are fleeting:

In the glory days of ancient Rome, victorious warriors returned to Rome in the midst of great fanfare and celebration. Large crowds gath-ered to cheer them as they rode into the city on chariots. But legend says that with them in their chariots also rode an aide carrying a sign reminding one and all that glory is fleeting.

Examples

Similar to anecdotes, examples or illustrations are the lifeblood of an article. How can you get across a point or lead up to a conclusion without the use of examples? General George S. Patton, the subject of the anecdote printed above, certainly understood the value of illustrating his point. Patton believed in doing what other lesser generals called impossible. He said, "The impossible is what we're in business for." As a leader of men, Patton had to convey this belief to thousands of soldiers and make them share his conviction. He backed up his statement with examples from history, such as the military strategy used by the Greeks and the Romans. Time and again, Patton cited history to make his points.

Patton's examples were powerful because they were from great military and wartime geniuses such as Julius Caesar and Alexander the Great.

Whenever you hear good speakers, in person or on television, watch for their use of examples. Speakers often give substance to their talks through the use of examples. The same is true for the articles you write; you can add new dimensions to your articles by using a variety of examples and illustrations.

Here are two examples from a published article titled "A Great Love Can Change Lives." Each illustration supports the premise of the article:

> Poet Robert Browning's love for his Elizabeth changed the face of all the world for her. He brought new joy into her sick world and taught her how wrong she was to be afraid to be happy. Her love for Robert gave her the strength to elope with him. And in so doing, she saved her own life and found a whole new world of joy, contentment, and meaning.
>
> The love of a little girl transformed the life of an old man named Silas Marner, in the immortal book. The lonely old man found the baby girl left on his doorstep and raised her as his own daughter. Thus a lonely miser's life was changed as his love for his daughter grew through the years and he came to realize how much more precious she was than the gold he counted and hoarded when he lived alone.

Notice how the stories work together to corroborate and strengthen the theme of the article. One example might be viewed as an isolated phenomena, but by including several, the author strengthens his case: The transformative power of love is universal.

Examples can take the form of case histories that drive home the point you are making. The author of the following excerpt wanted to convince readers that increasing their awareness of market needs could be both interesting and profitable:

> Starting a new business is a real challenge. Some have the ability to spot a need for a new business. One very alert entrepreneur, for example, saw that many toys for children don't call for any imagination. The toys do everything for the children.
>
> So what did this entrepreneur do about the missing link of imagination in many toys? She devised a series of creative toys that have no specific function—no battery-operated toys or electronic ones. One of her toys is simply a cardboard box. "Children can cut the box, paint it, or live in it." The toys her business offers children require and stimulate imagination.

Sources of Examples

Examples come from a variety of sources including:

- Daily news reports
- Your own personal experience
- Interviews with a variety of people
- Lives of famous people, as well as ordinary men and women
- Literature

Numbers Add Weight to Articles

Here's an example: "Of the 1,000 songs he has written, 538 have been published. Over 100 of them are songs instantly recognized and loved by people everywhere."

Why use numbers in an article? Because they add credibility and authenticity. Statistics add depth and substance to your articles and the stamp of authority. The importance of numbers cannot be overestimated. They back up the facts and statements made in an article and let the reader know that a writer's information is not just coming from the top of his or her head; there are specific numbers or percentages corroborating the points.

Simply think of numbers as underlying proof. Don't go overboard and create an article that reads like a statistics report, but some use of numbers definitely adds to the overall impressiveness of an article.

In an article by L. P. Wilbur, "The Silent Fields of Shiloh," the objective was to describe the awesome Civil War battlefield. Statistics were used to achieve this goal, but out of a thousand words, only three sentences actually included numbers:

> At the end of the first day of battle, Grant's forces were reduced to around 7,000. But during the night the weakened Union forces were reinforced by 25,000 fresh troops. Both North and South were greatly shocked by the amount of losses. The Confederates reported about 10,700 killed, wounded, captured, and missing. Union losses came to over 13,000.

The numbers used in the "Shiloh" article show the huge carnage of the battle. They thus reveal the tragedy of that battlefield for both sides and add credibility and overwhelming proof to the article. A great sense of loss is evident to the reader after digesting these numbers.

In an article about baseball great Lou Gehrig, numbers from his amazing record were quite useful. They were worked into the opening paragraph of the article: "fifteen years with the Yankees, a lifetime batting average of .341, played 2,130 consecutive major-league games, played in 7 World Series, and received the major league Best Player award four times."

The Gehrig record and numbers prove to the reader what a magnificent champion Lou Gehrig was, especially for that era. They stir the reader and show why this immortal player was so loved and is still remembered today.

Strive for a balanced blend of all the magic ingredients. For example, don't shortchange anecdotes or examples in favor of numbers. In time, you will develop sound judgment for the proper blending.

Quotations

Rarely do you see an effective article that has no quotes in it. Like statistics, quotes can add authority to your articles. They can also enhance your article with diversity, because they add the "own words" of someone other than yourself. Here is an example of the use of a quote:

The legendary Ray Kroc, the man who launched McDonald's, once said, "When I was a kid, I saw my dad struggling to make ends meet on a meager salary. I thought, If I could get a job that would guarantee me $10,000 a year, I'd sign a life contract."

That quote was very useful because it allowed the article writer to set up a strong and surprising contrast. The next sentence of the article reads: "Ray Kroc had the immense pleasure of seeing his onetime goal of $10,000 turn into millions."

Quotations add interest, background, information, and, above all, other points of view to your articles.

Sample Reports

If you can gain access to reports on some of the subjects you write articles about, you can add punch, power, and credibility to your work.

The use of sample reports shows the reader that you have done your homework; you have sought out other sources to explore the subject. Many such reports are done by experts, so your use of the material—within the rules of "fair use"—will add weight and help to persuade or convince the reader.

Say, for example, you are writing an article about the increased use of alcohol or tobacco among young people. Using selected statements and quotations from reports by experts will add real power to your article.

A good place to obtain such reports is the Government Printing Office. There may be charges for some of them, but some of them are free. Many reports can be downloaded for free from the Internet.

Comparisons or Contrasts

The use of comparisons and contrasts will enable your readers to see your point more quickly when reading your articles. The author of the following excerpt was writing about the universal human need for heroes.

When Sydney Carton, in Dicken's *A Tale of Two Cities*, was about to lose his head on the guillotine, his brave last words were certainly an inspiration to those who followed him. His words still have resonance in the hearts and spirits of all readers of the classic novel: "It is a far, far better thing I do, than I have ever done; it is a far, far better rest I go to, than I have ever known." Carton took another man's place at the guillotine, thus giving his life to save another innocent person.

A huge number of Americans just don't have anyone to look up to anymore. There are few heroes left these days.

The author reminds us of this well-known character from nineteenth-century fiction, and contrasts his final act of nobility against the lack of dignity and honor in real-world, twentieth-century America.

Should You Add Photographs, Sidebars, or Graphics?

Pictures can be valuable additions to your articles. To use an old cliché, One picture is worth a thousand words. That goes for illustrations, photographs, charts, etc. As we move into the twenty-first century, pictures will continue to play an important role in magazines, newspapers, newsletters, and the like. In fact, as publication software and photographic technology continue to improve and come down in price, illustrations may well become even more important. Many publishers of new media, such as Web 'zines, rely at least as much upon the picture as they do upon the word to get their message out.

Illustrations increase the overall effectiveness of an article. In their early years as writers, many begin to build files of photos on all kinds of subjects. They then have their own photo archive when they need a picture to accompany a specific article. Writers with decades of experience behind them often have a large picture collection to choose from.

Unless you can take your own pictures, and wish to do so, you will have to acquire them from others. Sources for illustration include historical societies, state commerce departments, library picture collections, and stock photo agencies. In many cases, you will have to pay for these pictures, and the cost and what you get for your money varies a lot. For example, stock photography agencies usually charge for the right to use a picture—that is, they will allow the picture to be published once, in a specific venue—but require that the actual physical image is ultimately returned to them.

Some publications will be thrilled at your initiative, and will gladly publish your pictures if your article is accepted. In some cases, if the photographs are unusual or difficult to get hold of, editors will pay more for a package that includes both the writing and the pictures. However, many publishers prefer to take care of all accompanying artwork themselves. Often, the editorial and art departments work together to choose and layout illustrations. In these cases, the article writer may make suggestions.

Should you include sidebars and charts, or other graphics? Certain categories of articles are right for sidebars. Many business related articles go well with sidebars. Diagrams, graphs, and charts can aid the communication process by providing a visual aid to illuminate statistics.

Writer Todd Krieger says, "Occasionally sidebars are asked for, but that is something which is explicitly laid out beforehand—prior to writing and submitting the final article."

Still, if you are not writing on assignment, you should experiment with planning and submitting different articles in different forms. Include photographs with some articles; use sidebars or graphics with others. Each article is a new situation, offering you creative choices.

Improving the Body

As you would expect, the body of an article is where most of the work is done. While the opening paragraphs state the subject of the article, and what the writer's angle on that subject will be, the body of the article presents the information and arguments that support the writer's theme. Here are brief summaries of the bodies of three successful articles. We include them in order to show you what information and techniques can be used to develop the body of an article.

"Sydney: Saturday City" was published in the *Rotarian* (the magazine of the Rotary Club). The purpose of this travel article is to convince readers that Sydney is an interesting and attractive destination. After introducing his topic, author Gavin Souter offers a historical background of Sydney. His use of specific anecdotes keeps it interesting, and also provides the reader with a context for understanding the next section, which contrasts historical Sydney with the modern city.

Souter writes vivid descriptions of Sydney's landmarks—Harbour Bridge, the Opera House, the wharves, the towers—and goes on to provide an overview of the contemporary city: population and real estate statistics, specific sights and attractions. He paints a singular picture of Sydney's two unique geographical features: the beach and the "bush."

By grounding his article in historical detail and providing factual information, Souter establishes his credibility. Through the use of knowledgeable and vivid descriptions, he sells the reader on an Australian vacation.

In "A Question of Honor" author Allan Sherman's premise is that honor is an undervalued quality nowadays. His purpose in this *Reader's Digest* article is to persuade readers that honor is still important. To prove his point, Sherman presents five short, true incidents in which honor played a critical role. The first story is "The Bathtub Navy," which is about the miracle of Dunkirk and how many lives were saved there. For the next story, the author jumps from Dunkirk to the site of the Kennedy assassination. The other three tales are also historical examples of honor. While these stories are based on facts, they are not merely dry accounts. Sherman fills them with colorful, evocative details, making the characters, settings, and emotions very real for the reader. The article is effective because the reader gets caught up in the stories, and the stories present clear and convincing portraits of honor.

The purpose of "What Farmers Think of Family Farms" is quite different than that of the previous two examples. Here the author is not attempting to sway the reader's opinion through the use of anecdotes, nor to influence the reader's vacation plans by presenting attractive sights. This *Farm Journal* article is purely factual. It contains the details of a survey conducted on farmers throughout the nation. The article is divided into four sections, and each section has its own subtitle and reports on a specific topic covered in the survey. The information is largely statistical, but also includes farmer's comments from various surveys. The article succeeds because it is well-organized, informative, and concise.

Here is a sample article titled, "Coca-Cola: The Soft Drink That Changed the World" by L. P. Wilbur. We've included the entire article so you can better examine how the body of the article relates to the other parts of the article.

Coca-Cola: The Soft Drink That Changed the World

When a pharmacist created a unique soft drink syrup back in May, 1886, he started a company that has introduced one innovation after another.

Countless millions the world over would never think of letting a day go by without a nice, cold bottle, can, or fountain drink of Coca-Cola.

Three founder-leaders were behind the launching, early growth, and development of the legendary soft drink: Dr. John S. Pemberton, Asa G. Candler, and Robert W. Woodruff. According to legend, Dr. Pemberton, a local pharmacist, created the unique syrup for Coca-Cola, on May, 1886, in a three-legged brass pot in his backyard.

He took some to nearby Jacob's Pharmacy, where it was judged "excellent" and quickly offered for sale, as a soda fountain drink, at five cents a glass.

Either by accident or on purpose, carbonated water was teamed with the syrup, and the result was a refreshing and delightful soft drink.

Frank M. Robinson was Dr. Pemberton's partner and bookkeeper. Robinson had a hunch that "two Cs would look well together in advertising," so he created the famous "Coca-Cola" and suggested it to Dr. Pemberton.

The first newspaper ad for the new soft drink soon appeared in the *Atlanta Journal*. Thirsty citizens of Atlanta were invited to try the new soda fountain drink. Signs advertising "Coca-Cola" began appearing on store awnings, and the word "Drink" was added to let people know it was for soda fountain enjoyment. Sales in that first year averaged just 9 drinks a day.

Unfortunately, Dr. Pemberton never realized the great potential of the syrup-beverage he created. He slowly sold portions of his business to partners. Just before his death, in 1888, he sold the rest of his interest in Coca-Cola to Asa G. Candler, a noted Atlantan with keen business insight. Candler bought additional rights and gained complete control.

Candler soon ran a full-page ad announcing that his wholesale-retail drug business was "sole proprietor of Delicious, Refreshing, Exhilarating, Invigorating Coca-Cola." Incredibly, gaining full control by 1891, the Coca-Cola Company cost Candler a total of $2,300.

Within a year of acquiring sole ownership, Candler's talent for merchandising had increased sales by almost tenfold. Seeing this growth, Candler put all his attention on Coca-Cola. He formed The Coca-Cola Company with his brother, John S. Candler, Frank Robinson (Dr. Pemberton's former partner) and two other associates.

The "Coca-Cola" trademark was registered in the U.S. Patent Office on January 31, 1893. During the same year, Coca-Cola paid its first dividend of $20 per share. Every year since then, dividends have been paid on the common stock of the company.

The first syrup manufacturing plant outside Atlanta opened in Dallas in 1894. And the next year, 1895, Candler announced that "Coca-Cola is now available in every state and territory in the United States."

A man in Vicksburg, Mississippi, Joseph A. Biedenharn, saw such a demand at his soda fountain for Coca-Cola that he installed bottling machinery in the back of his store. In this way, he was able to start selling cases of Coca-Cola to various lumber camps and plantations up and down the Mississippi River. He was the first bottler of the Coca-Cola soft drink.

Bottling on a large scale began in 1899 when rights were obtained from Candler to bottle and sell Coca-Cola throughout the United States. Within the next 20 years, the number of bottling plants grew to more than 1,000, with 95% of them locally owned and operated. In the early years of the century, bottlers stayed busy protecting Coca-Cola from imitation. This was reflected in advertising phrases like "Demand the genuine," and "Accept no substitute."

The Candler interests sold The Coca-Cola Company, in 1919, to Atlanta banker Ernest Woodruff and an investor group. The price was $25 million.

Some four years later, Robert Winship Woodruff, Ernest's son, became president and led Coca-Cola for more than six decades.

As the new leader and president, Robert Woodruff focused on product quality. He launched a team of well-trained servicemen to help fountain outlets to actively sell and correctly serve Coca-Cola.

Woodruff's management took Coca-Cola to new heights of success. The innovative six-bottle carton was started in the early 1920s and soon became one of the industry's most powerful merchandising tools. In 1929, the metal, open-top collar was introduced, which made it possible for Coca-Cola to be served ice-cold in retail outlets.

Woodruff's major contribution was his idea and vision of Coca-Cola as an international product. With his associates, Woodruff established the global momentum that brought Coca-Cola to every corner of the world.

Points to Remember

- The body of your article should support your theme.

- Anecdotes can illustrate a point or an event.

- The use of statistics, reports, examples, and quotes show the reader that you have done your homework.

- The body of your article may be divided into sections, through the use of subheads.

- Most readers like, and expect, a variety of ingredients in the articles they read (anecdotes, illustrations, facts, quotations, and numbers).

Practice Exercises

1. List three anecdotes you would use in an article on the massive challenge of running for president of the United States.

2. Find three memorable quotations. Put them on file cards for future reference and possible use.

3. Look at the middle part of the last article you wrote, then try to improve it.

4. Read three new articles this week. Figure out what tactics the authors used to develop the bodies of the articles.

5. Study the body of an article you have written. Decide if you could add subheads and break the article into several sections.

Interviews Add Credibility to Your Words

It's entirely possible to write articles without doing any interviews, but in most cases, interview material adds a strong dimension to articles on almost any subject. Readers want to hear the ideas, opinions, and observations of others, particularly if these views come from respected authorities.

Advantages of Interviewing

Let's take a look at the advantages of doing interviews when planning and writing your articles.

- Interviewing will teach you to be selective. You will often get more material in an interview than can be used, and judgment must be used in selecting what to include.

- Interviews and material based on interviews add credibility to your articles. The ideas of those interviewed will support what is stated in an article. In addition, the reader appreciates that the writer has sought people in the know on the subject, meaning it's not just what the writer thinks.

- Conducting a number of interviews also increases a writer's self-confidence. You are more assured about the accuracy of an article when you know that you have talked to a dozen or more people on the subject. Interviews are part and parcel of the writing business. They provide a welcome break from the computer or word processor, and these breaks can also stimulate new article ideas. You will discover that during your interviews, ideas for brand-new articles will flood your mind.

A writer friend we know once interviewed the manager of a local college bookstore for a trade journal article. In the course of getting the information on how she ran the store, the writer came up with six new article ideas. They were later developed into full-length articles on related subjects and sold to national publications. Here are the ideas that were realized due to that one interview:

- "The College Bookstore of Tomorrow"
- "Supervising Student Employees"
- "See Yourself as a Sales Specialist"
- "What It Means to Manage a Bookstore"
- "It Pays to Follow Your Selling Hunches"
- "Selling in Fair Weather or Foul"

A writer's communicative abilities often will be sharpened through interviews. Remember, it is not just the interviewee who must communicate; it is the writer's job to ask the right questions and to keep the person talking and focused. A great many writers sit alone in their studies, at their desks, in lonely rooms, cabins, or wherever they do their work. Over a period of time, their conversational skills can suffer. Interviewing consistently helps to keep a writer able to communicate in a professional way.

Another big plus is that the individuals that a writer interviews may be able to suggest some excellent sources for additional material on the subject. They can sometimes help you obtain photos or even supply them themselves on occasion. By interviewing a tour guide at a Beverly Hills mansion, where a great film star lived most of his life, L. P. Wilbur obtained some fine additional information and a complete set of high-quality photos of the estate. This extra material made for a much stronger overall article.

Still another considerable advantage is the fact that some of those you interview may become friends and future sources for points of view, quotes, and other material. There may even be occasions when one of them can recommend you to various publications for article assignments.

Whenever you consider article ideas, be sure to think about the interview possibilities. Keep in mind also that the more interviews you do, the more skilled you become. If you wish to tape-record your interviews, remember to ask permission first.

How to Conduct an Article Interview

Your first objective in this process is to set up the interview. This can be done by requesting an appointment by telephone, e-mailing a request, or faxing or sending a written request. If you cannot reach the person directly, you might have to contact their business manager, public relations agent, or personal manager—especially if the person is a celebrity.

In your first communication, be sure to explain your background and the nature of the article you are doing. State how and why you feel an interview with the person would be of help to you. Be specific about what you wish to cover during the interview. Mention your published work.

Assuming that your interview request is granted, the second step is to prepare for the meeting. This can be accomplished in the following ways:

- Read any available background material on the person you are going to interview. If there is a biography on him or her, read it.

- Read her works, if any, to learn about her hobbies, interests, career goals, achievements, and more.

- If the person you're interviewing is a celebrity, it often helps to talk to his or her friends, relatives, or family members as well, if possible.

- Your next step is to prepare a list of key questions to use during the interview. That will give you a specific track to run on and a plan. When preparing the list of questions, take the time to phrase each one well; the quality of the answers often depends on the quality of the questions. A vague or confusing question may bring the same kind of answer.

Let the person being interviewed talk at will. In fact, many writers don't use prepared questions, unless the person being interviewed is uncommunicative. The questions can then be used as a tool for encouraging the person to open up. Some people are more talkative than others; you will run into many types, and it's nice to have key questions on hand when you need them.

You should know in advance whether to rely on taking notes to get the material you need or to tape-record the entire meeting. If you do lots of interviews, you will most likely use both methods. When an interview is granted, that's a good time to ask, "Would it be okay to bring my tape recorder so I can be sure to quote you accurately?" If the person you are interviewing objects to a recording, then you must rely on your note taking.

If you do tape-record an interview, it is common courtesy to let your subject read, and possibly edit, the transcript. Your interview subjects may talk much more freely in the session if they feel that they won't be held to every word. Some writers are afraid that their subjects will want to cut out a juicy topic of conversation from the interview, so they will not let their subjects read any material—transcript or draft of the article—until the press date. The choice is yours, but know that you could be risking "bad blood" between you and your interviewee.

Here's another important guideline: If a person you are interviewing tells you something "off the record," do *not* use it in the article. Always respect the wishes of those you interview, or you risk losing their trust, respect, and future cooperation on any other articles.

Do your very best in every single interview to quote the person accurately. Being misquoted irritates and angers most people and makes future interviews with them unlikely.

Whenever you do an in-depth profile—usually of a film star, celebrity, or sports figure—you will probably need a series of interviews with the person to get all the information you require. If this is the case, try to get the person's okay to follow him through his daily routine for a day or two in the office, at home, on location, etc. The more information you obtain, the better the choice of material you will have for the article.

Take the time to read some of the excellent in-depth interviews of film stars and celebrities. There are many magazines that specialize in this subject. *Premiere* magazine, *Entertainment Weekly*, and *People* magazine are three mainstream publications that come to mind. You can also log online and use a search engine such as Yahoo!, Excite, or Infoseek to filter through the thousands of articles available to view (for free) over the Internet.

If you do get the opportunity to interview celebrities, make sure you do your homework. Writer and editor Roy Frumkes, who has conducted countless celebrity interviews, cautions: "This is the era of interviews; the plethora of media demands constant sound bites from high-profile people. Interviewees are easily tired, and fall into repeating familiar tales that have already been told to previous interviewers. If you can surprise them, you can come up with something unique."

Here's another simple preparation Frumkes never neglects, which quite often ensures that the interview begins on the right foot. "I always come armed with props—notebook, camera, tape recorder, of course, but also personal mementos—photos from the actor's current movie, production stills from the director's first film, a copy of the writer's least-known novel, anything that shows I've gone beyond the basic call of the job. I want to get the interviewees talking, get them excited."

As the number of your interviews increase, strive to develop the ability to ask provocative, probing questions. Many writers find this difficult to do. Some of the key people on television have the ability to ask painful questions.

You will have to decide when and if to ask especially tough questions. The person you are interviewing may or may not answer, but remember, too, that you can always rephrase and soften tough questions if they don't work at first.

Points to Remember

- Conducting interviews provides welcome breaks from the computer, as well as new article ideas.
- Interviews upgrade articles and add substance and credibility to their total impact.
- Advance preparation for an interview is a must.
- Many who grant interviews prefer not to be recorded, but a writer can always ask permission to use a tape recorder in order to quote the person as accurately as possible.

- If the person being interviewed is not talkative, use a list of previously prepared questions.

- The ability and willingness to ask tough questions can pay off with a stronger article.

Practice Exercises

1. Decide on an article you would like to write. Request one or more interviews with people in your local area who are connected to the subject, or who may be able to provide you with information.

2. Examine two or three of your finished articles. Ask yourself if one or more of them could have been improved or made more effective by the use of interview material.

3. Conduct an interview using this chapter as a guide. Then write a one-paragraph summary of what you learned from doing the interview.

4. If you're a veteran writer with a number of published articles, ask yourself how you might streamline or improve your present interview methods.

How to Sell Your Articles

It is tougher to sell articles today than it used to be, for a number of reasons. One of the main reasons is that editors have a much larger choice of material. Everyone and his brother's cousin, sister, and friends are writing. This vastly increases the competition for all writers—the veteran pros who have been at it for decades, as well as newcomers.

A Few Words Concerning Editors

In the opinion of the authors of this book, there are three basic types of editors today: great, mediocre, and bad. The four-star, dedicated, and highly professional editor is the very best to work with for a number of reasons:

- The editor responds promptly to proposals and queries.
- The editor welcomes new article ideas and willingly communicates interest in seeing either an outline or a finished article.
- The editor treats writers with respect and courtesy.
- The editor lets you know what the status of an article is and when it is likely to be published.

- The editor is willing to work with a writer regarding any changes or rewrites. An excellent editor will make suggestions that will actually improve the article, while respecting the writer's vision.

- The editor sees that the writer is paid on time.

There are other traits that define the best type of editor, but the above ones are some of the major qualities.

A mediocre editor is simply less professional. He or she takes longer to respond to query letters, is perhaps annoyed if a writer phones to pitch an idea or check on an article, and is less courteous to writers. A mediocre editor may not be very good at seeing a writer's vision.

Finally, the third type of editor is rude, uncaring, does not reply to communication of any kind, returns articles with staples in them rather than paper-clipped, can never be pleased, soils articles with coffee or other stains, goes ballistic if a writer telephones, and may hold one or more articles for a year or longer. Yes, it has happened and does. Unfortunately, there are nasty people in positions of power in the publishing trade, just as in every other industry. All writers, certainly those who have been at it for a period of years or longer, have horror stories about some editors.

This is not to say that all editors are bad. On the contrary, most are highly professional and caring. Again, just as in any other business, some appear to be neglectful simply because they are so overwhelmed by work. (Remember, if the competition is stiffer, it also means that editors have to make their way through a lot more manuscripts.)

The late John Gardner, who was a successful novelist and article writer, taught writing at a university in Iowa and wrote several definitive books on the subject, stated the following: "Most editors are either incompetent or crazy." While we don't completely agree with the statement, it's not hard to understand why writers end up feeling this way. After all, editors have the authority to reject the writer's words, which not only makes them arbiters of taste—they decide what's fit to print—but also gives them power over the writer's economic health (if they don't buy, the author's wallet remains thin). In addition, editors usually change or cut at least some of the writer's hard-found words, and not always with the greatest sensitivity or diplomacy.

Still, we prefer to think most editors try their best to be professional. If you stay in this profession over time, you will probably encounter all three types of editors. If you have a bad experience with someone who ignores you or disrespects either you or your writing, you should simply cross him or her off your list. If you connect with editors of the first type, stick with them, at all costs.

Know Your Markets

Many writers focus on knowing the markets and take their chances that most publications will have good editors at the helm. You take your chances as an article writer, just as you do in other careers and vocations.

By knowing the markets, we don't mean giving them a quick glance once a week or a few times a month. The real pro article writers are studying markets every single day, or at least six days a week. Not the entire day, mind you, but devoting a block of time regularly to keeping up.

Markets change constantly. Magazines are snuffed out almost daily, while flocks of new ones are just taking flight. We can sense your question: So how does a writer keep up with them? Here are proven steps that have worked, and are working, for many pro writers:

1. Subscribe to at least some of your favorite magazine and other markets and especially those you hope and expect to write for in the future. If there is no way you can subscribe, then look each issue over whenever possible.

2. Make it your business to go by a good-sized library a few times (or more) weekly and go immediately to the periodical room. There, in most large libraries, you will find many kinds of current magazines on shelves, usually arranged alphabetically. You can study them free this way, without having to pay a cent. This step will not help you much unless you hit that periodical room consistently—several times each and every week.

   You will find journals and also newsletters, as well as magazines and newspapers, in the periodical room. We recommend university libraries, because they often subscribe to hundreds and hundreds of publications. You could spend six months or a year in some of these huge rooms and still not see everything. Who knows? There are probably some writers who have vanished in those enormous stacks.

3. Contact the publications you want to sell to and request a sample copy. Unfortunately, most of them today will charge you for the sample, but there are still some that are gracious enough to send a free copy. The problem is that so many requests are now received for sample copies that publications have no choice but to start charging.

   Study the sample copies you do receive and take notes on the kind of articles being used, the format of the publication, and the types of advertisers. Read through the articles in each issue. This way you get a feel for the style and flavor of each magazine.

4. Learn the market categories. A good way to do this is to study the table of contents of *Writer's Market*. You will see all the categories listed—general magazines, fraternal, young adult, teen markets, religious, scientific, farming publications, and so on. By using the *Writer's Market*, you will save yourself time and effort; you won't make the mistake of submitting a celebrity profile to a publisher of scientific journals, for example. Pros rarely err through mismatching their articles with the wrong type of market. Newcomers need to learn how to avoid this as soon as possible.

   As you become more experienced, you should begin to write with specific markets in mind. You will learn not to focus on an article unless or until you can list five or six markets for it. Some ideas don't seem right for any markets. Put those on the back burner. They will simmer in your subconscious, and eventually your brain may boil over with ideas for where to market them and what angle to write them from. In the meantime, give your conscious attention to article ideas that have the widest chance for seeing print and that are right for a number of markets.

   The pros in this business have learned how to slant an article for different markets. They redo the article, or simply knock out a new version, using the same information, only with minor changes.

5. Do your homework on the publications you are targeting. Learn their submission policies (both e-mail and snail mail), editor's names, and all other pertinent information. This can be accomplished by visiting your local newsstand armed with

a pen and paper, then thumbing through your favorite publications and writing down the information you need. You can also access the Internet and tap into a wealth of resources. The Writers' Guidelines Database, for example, is one of the largest guides to paying, nonfiction publications on the Web (*http://mav.net/guidelines/*) with more than three hundred guidelines in their database.

6. You cannot sell an article again if you have sold all the rights to it. If you sell "first rights," then you still own and can sell the second rights or reprint rights to that article. There are many markets that will buy onetime rights to an article. In that case, you can offer the article again to other markets.

   Keep up with which rights were sold on each of your articles. You can do this by keeping a record book or noting the rights sold, and date, on an index card each time you make a sale. Be sure to note the title of the article and which market purchased it.

7. One final reminder regarding markets: Don't forget about overseas markets. One of your articles might collect rejection slips from American editors and then sell the first time out to a Canadian magazine or a London newspaper syndicate. Market knowledge can mean the difference between your success and failure. You might be a talented writer, but you will fail if you do not study the markets. It is an absolute must.

How to Test Your Ideas before Submitting Them

There are several very helpful guidelines that will enable you to test your article ideas before sending them off to market. Here they are:

- Is the idea big enough? Is it strong enough?

- Would enough readers be interested? Does your article idea offer help for the reader or stimulate enough interest?

- Are you the right writer for it? In truth, what you are asking yourself here is: Do you want to write it? If the subject bores you, or you can't muster enough interest and desire to write it (or to do the research and set up the interviews), then you should move on to a better idea for you.

- Are there at least five or six markets for it? If you only see two or three likely markets, it might be wiser to choose another idea where the market potential is stronger.

Use the questions above as a guide, for they have helped many professionals for a long time. You want your articles to be accepted and published so people can enjoy reading them and learning from them. To achieve that purpose, you need to focus on the best ideas that you believe have the greatest chance to work.

Submissions to Editors and the Editorial Process

As stated earlier, most editors will treat you fairly, provided you send your articles in the accepted manner. This means neat presentations, on computer or word processor, with your name and address in the upper left corner and the approximate number of words in the upper right corner of the first page.

We can almost guarantee that if you do not provide for the return of your work—meaning the standard SASE (self-addressed, stamped envelope)—you have seen the last of it. Unfortunately, some editors do not return material, even though the writer provided the return postage and envelope.

If and when you become well established as a writer, with a big enough name, you may be able to omit the SASE. It's hard to imagine a star writer (Steven King, perhaps?) enclosing a SASE. There is the point of view that holds that an SASE invites rejection. Our advice? Until you have made a big name for yourself as an article writer, the better part of wisdom is to enclose a SASE.

Since you will probably write your article on a computer, you don't really have to worry about your only copy of an article being lost on an editor's desk; you can always print out another copy to submit elsewhere. (Make sure you never submit an original manuscript; always have it photocopied or saved to a disk). Still, if you send the SASE, it is much more likely that the editor will communicate with you, either with a form rejection or perhaps with some words of encouragement or interest. It is better to get definitive feedback than to have the sense that one is just pitching proposals out into an empty void.

Will your article be edited? It will be, if necessary. Many editors expect the writer to send material that needs little or no editing, which may have influenced them to buy in the first place. Editors at most publications are simply too busy to edit every article substantially. They may possibly suggest a few changes, such as a different title, a change in a section, or they may request that the article be cut or expanded. Each editor has his or her own methods and ideas. As the writer, you will usually be asked to approve any substantive changes. You should know that the publication itself probably has a "house style"—a way in which that particular venue handles issues of grammar, spelling, and style—and your writing, if accepted, will definitely be edited to conform to it.

Some editors may ask to see an outline of your idea before giving you the go-ahead. When this happens, the editor may offer guidance regarding the structure of the outline and the development of the article. This is a strong signal that the editor really likes your idea and will work with you on fleshing it out. In my experience, this occurs now and then, but not often. Most editors are far too busy.

Working styles of editors vary, but one common trait most of them share is a dislike of phone calls from writers. You can see why. If five or ten writers call them on a given morning or afternoon, that's five or ten interruptions to the process of reading and editing. Better to write, or to e-mail, your queries.

Some editors will reply very professionally on their publication's letterheads. Some will react to new ideas with thoughtful letters. Others will scribble notes on your query letter in the margins or at the bottom of the page.

A New York business magazine editor I have done a lot of articles for reached the point where anything not sent in on a floppy disk was automatically rejected. Some editors today demand computerized material, e-mail queries, and fax communications. These editors have kissed snail mail goodbye for all time to come. Fortunately, a number of editors still consider traditional letters and hard-copy manuscripts, even sometimes preferring that nothing be sent on a disk. But as time passes, and technology continues to take over the world, expect the total demise of the envelope letter accompanying the neatly typed-on-bond-paper manuscript.

If an editor accepts your article, and then asks you to rethink and rewrite it, you will probably not receive any extra money for the additional work you do. However, a thorough check of the current markets reveals that many publications offer a writer more money—often a lot more, or even double—if the article is assigned, as opposed to merely accepted. In this scenario, you would submit a proposal, as opposed to a completed article, to a market. If the idea found favor with the editor, he would ask you to go ahead with it. If the editor accepted your finished article, you would most likely receive the amount, or range, stated in the publication's market information. Unsolicited articles usually bring in a lot less money.

Most editors will see that you receive a check for your material, along with copies of the issue containing your article. It is, of course, better financially for a writer to work with markets that pay on acceptance. However, many markets still pay on publication, which means the writer has to wait two or three months or longer for his money and, in a few cases, six months or a year.

When you study market listings, you will sometimes see "kill fees" stated. This means that if the editor fails to use your piece, or kills it after expressing interest in it and accepting it, you will receive the standard amount offered by that publication as a kill fee. Some of the larger, well-known magazines and markets offer such kill fees. They help to pay for at least some of a writer's time and effort, in the event your material is not published.

Query the Editor First

Love 'em or hate 'em, most of today's busy editors insist that writers query them prior to sending any article submissions. Since they say to query first, that means a writer must craft a short, snappy letter and e-mail or snail mail it to the editor. Submissions by regular mail must include a return stamped envelope. (Warning: Some editors will reject your unsolicited query, even if it is hand delivered by a Tyra Banks look-alike.)

The first step remains the query. Getting the editor to read and consider it, and respond, can be tough. The best advice—and all the pros have been long aware of it—is to keep *lots* of queries out there at all times. We know article writers who consistently keep a whopping forty or more article queries circulating to editors. In other words, they play the numbers game. With that many queries out, they are always getting back some go-aheads and assignments from editors.

Other writers cope with the problem by contacting only those editors they have worked with previously and whom they know will get back to them promptly.

If an editor does not reply to your query letter in a reasonable length of time, even though you enclosed the SASE, what do you do?

Give the editor the benefit of the doubt and write once more, requesting the status of the article. Or try phoning and asking about your article. If there is still no reply, cross that editor off your list and try another one. Please also note this fact: Many editors go bonkers if a writer dares to telephone them. Others do not mind being called. Try to find out how a given editor feels about it.

If your article comes back with torn edges, stains, and other signs of ill treatment, when you know you sent the neatest original, you would be wise to eliminate that editor from your list. Don't blame the editor, however, if you sent out a sloppy, worn-looking article. It is your job to send the neatest and most professional submissions possible.

How to Write a Query Letter with Impact

What exactly is an article query? It's an idea for an article submitted to an editor in letter form. A query allows a writer to find out if there is a demand for his article idea before writing it. A writer might also use a query letter to promote interest in an article that has already been completed, but which has not yet been sold to a publisher.

What's the secret to writing an effective query letter? There is no single, right way to craft a query, but there are some basic guidelines you should follow. Limit your query to a single, easy-to-read page, if at all possible. State your idea, how you propose to handle the subject, your sources of information, what sections or areas the article will explore, and the anticipated, or actual, length. If you can, send any photos and perhaps a working title. Try to craft a letter that showcases your individuality without appearing cute. Make sure your grammar is perfect, and always address your query letter to a specific person by name and title. Some writers like to include an overview of their qualifications, or even attach a résumé of writing credits.

Another option is to send an outline of the article you have in mind. Include a cover letter. The outline would present the main parts or section headings of the article and what the material under each section would consist of. Simply give the editor a logical breakdown of what would be included in the article and present this information in outline form. (For an example of outline form, look at "The Outline" section of chapter 6.)

Your cover letter with this option need only state that you would like to write an article on the subject, that you are enclosing an outline for the article, the length you plan, and a title, if any. Remember that you are trying to intrigue the editor and get her to ask for more; you don't want to overwhelm her with words or information.

A third way to query is to send the actual beginning of your article, so the editor can see its style and direction. This type of query may whet an editor's curiosity, for it gives him an opportunity to see only how the article will begin. If the beginning "clicks" for the editor, you will get a go-ahead to send the rest of the article.

A number of writers do not bother to query editors. They write their articles and send copies of them to markets unsolicited. In today's article business, however, this may be a wasted effort. The editorial departments of many publications will not read unsolicited manuscripts. If you send your article, rather than a query, to such markets, your manuscript will probably not be read, and it may not be returned, either. Occasionally, you will find a market that says to send the manuscript, but it is less and less likely.

What editors look for in your query is evidence that the resulting article will be a solid and effective piece of work. In many cases, the markets you plan to query can supply guidelines as to what format your query should take, as well as what general subject categories they are interested in. For example, the editors of the *Write Markets Report* say this to potential queriers:

> We are seeking articles on various ways for writers to make money from their writing (i.e., unique assignments, corporate services, self-publishing, marketing, and networking advice, alternative products and services that writers can pursue and sell). Pay $50 for first rights, $30 for reprints for articles to 600 words. Submit query and credits by e-mail or by mail with SASE. E-mail queries to *aadair@electrotex.com*.

To convince an editor that your article will pass the test, try to get the following ingredients into your query:

- Tout your article's newness and freshness. Editors are not likely to be interested if there are many other recently published articles on the subject. Check the *Reader's Guide to Periodic Literature* in your library to see what has already been done on the subject.

- Many editors these days ask for published clips of previous articles you have done. If none are sent with the query, some editors automatically rule out that writer, even though they may be making an error.

- If you do send published clips, or "tearsheets," of your previous articles, know that you will not get them back. It seems to us that some editors care more about getting and building a supply of clips than they do about the articles sent in by writers. Maybe they throw them all in a thick file for future reference. Then, when they need article ideas, they simply glance through their backlog of clips. Who knows?

Remember also that you can upgrade and streamline your query by rewriting it. Never underestimate the importance of rethinking, revamping, and polishing anything that you have written. You can also take old queries and update them, inject new slants and directions into them, and then try new editors (or old ones) with them.

Sample Query Letters

Here are a few sample query letters:

Sample Query Letter #1

Dear :

Please consider the attached article, "Killer Microbots," for inclusion in your magazine.

My writing history dates back the early 1980s when my first article was published in *Omni* magazine. I have continued to write articles related to science and technology, and my most recent articles appeared in the January 1999 issue of *Maxim* and the May 1999 issue of *Wired* magazines.

I am interested in selling onetime rights, if possible.

Additionally, I am open to serialization of my forthcoming novel, *Beyond Dolly: The Race to Create the World's First Virtual Human Lifeform*.

I hope you will accept the article and inform your readership about the latest advances in microtechnology, which many science professionals find so intriguing.

Sincerely yours,

Sample Query Letter #2

Dear :

I am a freelance writer and novice wine connoisseur residing in Napa Valley, California. My articles have appeared in such magazines as *Cigar Aficionado, Maxim,* and *GQ;* I am also the author of three travel books about the Napa Valley and Calistoga area.

I am writing to suggest a humor article titled, "The Bachelor's Guide to Wine." A portion of the article is based on hypothetical interviews with single guys trying to impress women with their expansive knowledge of wine. It's quite an entertaining read!

I think you will find my writing style original and humorous—and a good match with your target readers. The length of the article is approximately 1,500 words.

I'll be glad to send this article at your request. A return envelope is enclosed.

I look forward to hearing from you soon.

Cheers,

Sample Query Letter #3

Dear :

On a recent trip to Memphis, Tennessee, I interviewed the General Manager of the famous Peabody Hotel. I picked up some very good quotes on his management style—ways to increase business, coming trends, and much more. With your okay, I'd be happy to send you a 1,200-word article based on my interview.

I await your reply to send the article and I very much look forward to working with your professional journal.

Sincerely yours,

For more information on writing an effective query letter, you may want to invest in Lisa Collier Cool's well-written book, *How to Write Irresistible Query Letters* (Writer's Digest Books).

Submitting Your Article: Paper, E-mail, or Floppy Disk?

As the new years of a new century unfold, editors will no doubt want to see more articles sent in e-mail form or on floppy disk. If the old familiar paper submission is phasing out, what choice do you have but to make the editor happy and ship your articles in by fax, e-mail, or disk?

A true story: Recently an author faxed about a third of his book manuscript to one of New York's hotshot literary agents. The agent herself received the fax, read the material, and requested the rest of the manuscript. It was faxed. The result was a book deal with a large amount of up-front money for the author.

The point is that faxes, floppy disks, and e-mail are in, while snail mail is about to bite the dust. If you do build a career as an article writer, you will have to submit your materials in the formats the industry requires. And you should know that not every market will ask for the same format. For example, many editors still prefer to read and work on a hard copy of your submission, although they usually ask for a computer file as well. We live in a changing world, and it's stupid to go against the grain. No doubt there were many who believed that the telephone, when it first arrived on the world scene, was either silly or "a tool of the devil."

A Little Luck Never Hurts

Veteran writers know that the longer you are in the writing business, the better your chance for a little luck to swing your way. It's true.

Keep enough queries winging their way (however you send them), write enough articles, make them as strong and interesting as possible, slant them for the best markets, and keep at it, and all of this has a way of working in your favor.

There is a law of averages, and it definitely works for writers, as well as others. Step up to the plate often enough with your articles, offer enough of them to enough editors, and sooner or later, you are going to hit your share of home runs.

We like to think of this little saying: Happy is the man who has found his work; let him ask no other blessing. If article writing is the right vocation for you, it will not be a chore for you to persevere, because the process of writing itself will bring you joy. And if you keep at it, keep doing what you love to do, there is a good chance that you will succeed.

Selling Your Articles to Overseas Markets

Many writers limit their article work to American markets only, and thus miss the opportunity to sell some of their work to markets in England, Australia, Scotland, Germany, Japan, and other countries. Though it's not overseas, Canadian markets also buy articles.

Overseas markets can mean extra sales for you. Once you gain experience in sending articles to magazines, newspapers, and syndicates in other countries, you will realize the potential is limitless. Overseas markets may in time account for a quarter or more of your article income.

Go through your idea files and copies of all your articles, and look for information or material that would interest overseas editors. Then also write a new version of selected articles, slanting them for the readers in other countries.

There are any number of subjects, events, and personalities in your native country that would be of interest to readers overseas. In fact, you will sometimes stand a better chance of selling such articles to various markets overseas than to publications at home.

If an article you write has international appeal, you might be able to sell it to markets in a number of countries. An excellent example of this is the glut of articles that appeared after the death of Elvis Presley. Millions in countries all over the world wanted to read the follow-up articles about the hordes of fans who went to Memphis to visit the Presley grave.

Political scandals are also fit subjects for overseas markets. Millions of people in other nations like to know what is going on in the United States. Don't limit yourself, consider the world market a part of your sales territory.

Some foreign publications actually pay more than the homegrown ones. One author of this book sold a number of articles to an Australian magazine. The checks were larger than many American markets would have paid, and the reply-response time was faster, too.

Here's an idea that has worked for a number of writers interested in selling work to overseas markets. Try spending Monday through Friday of each week getting articles off to markets in this country, and devoting weekends to submitting articles to a variety of overseas markets. Or simply send at least a small percentage of your work to markets in other countries.

Editors in other countries, just like editors at home, often require a query first, so you will have to keep firing off queries to overseas publications. That means a higher postage cost in many cases, but if you get a larger check for your work, it will balance out.

There is something very refreshing about working with overseas markets and editors. Many of them, you will discover, are more professional and courteous with writers than those in your native land.

Keeping up with foreign magazines and newspapers allows you to see what kinds of articles are being written and published around the globe. You can gain insight into the editorial policy of distant markets and see how various subjects are being treated in different countries. All in all, the experience of working with an international mix of editors is bound to make you a better writer.

What other benefits are there waiting for you in offering your work to editors overseas? How about prestige? Sales to foreign markets add to your track record and reputation as a writer. It's nice to know that you have been published in England, Japan, Australia, Germany, Italy, France, Switzerland, Scotland, and Canada, to name a few possibilities. When American editors learn that you have a list of published credits overseas, most of them will be impressed and, perhaps, more likely to use your work. It's very strong proof that a variety of publishers like your work and are using it on a regular basis. In addition, your visibility as a writer will increase because more editors will see your articles and bylines in publications of their countries.

DISADVANTAGES OF SELLING TO OVERSEAS MARKETS

To give you both sides of the picture, you need to know that there are some disadvantages in selling your work overseas. The advantages outweigh these drawbacks, but you will have to make the final decision on whether to offer your work to foreign editors.

One drawback is the fact that it takes longer to hear from some overseas markets because of the distance. Remember, we said earlier that some of these foreign editors will get back to you more quickly than those in your own nation. But others will take longer.

Another drawback is that some checks from overseas publications may be greeted with strange looks at your bank. It may take your bank some time to clear checks drawn on foreign banks.

Another, minor, negative is the fact that you cannot use regular American stamps for your SASE. You must enclose international coupons for this purpose, which you can buy from your post office.

Of course, you may be able to fax your articles to many of these foreign markets, but the cost will be higher.

ADVANTAGES OUTWEIGH DISADVANTAGES

The positive considerations for selling articles to overseas markets overshadow the negative ones. If you plan to offer your work to overseas markets, you need a copy of *Artists and Writers International Book*, which is published yearly and is known by many as the "red book" (for its cover). The leading magazine and newspaper markets for many countries are listed in each new edition.

Listed below are some foreign markets, including some of the leading ones, that may interest you. Be warned: editors, e-mail addresses, etc., change *quickly*. For the most up-to-the-minute information you will need a current copy of *Artists and Writers International Book*, or better still, Internet access to the Online Media Directory, published by The Editor and Publisher Company (*www.mediainfo.com/emedia*).

Some Leading Foreign Market Publications

Annabel (Today's magazine for today's woman); London
Animal World; London
Christian Herald (Britain's popular Christian family paper)
Country Life; London
The *Daily Telegraph*; London
The *Daily Mirror*; London
This England; London
Illustrated London News; London
The *Lady* (Weekly newspaper)
The *Sun* (London newspaper)
The *London Times* (newspaper)
Punch Magazine; London
My Weekly; London

How to Deal with Rejection Letters

Rejection slips can be depressing, especially if you are just starting out. Remember, even top professional writers get rejections sometimes, although not nearly as many as they did at the beginning of their careers.

One of the best ways to cope with rejections is simply to view them as the natural part of paying your dues. Every person who tries his hand at article writing receives them. They are a hazard of the trade. Some writers devise clever things to do with their rejection slips. One writer covered the walls of his home with them. Another writer wrote and sold an article on all the different ways an editor could say no to a writer—all the different reasons why an article could be turned down.

Most writers grow used to rejection slips. They know that the law of averages means some rejections for every sale made. No writer who turns out a healthy number of articles sells all of his or her work, and some of the finest articles ever written were rejected by any number of editors before seeing print.

Whenever you get a rejection slip, think of it as just one person's point of view. Other editors may feel differently and accept your article. Sometimes articles are rejected for reasons that are beyond the control of the writer. Maybe the editor had a fight with his or her spouse or got up on the wrong side of the bed. Maybe she perused your article when she was too tired to give it her full attention. Editors have their bad days, just like everyone else. Maybe the magazine received ten queries on the same topic this month. It happens.

There is another psychological step you can take. Try laughing out loud every time you get a rejection slip for an article. Then, post haste—and we mean pronto—get that article, or query, off to another editor.

Some articles sell the first time they are submitted. Others will sell on the second, third, or tenth try. Some need to sit in the back of your filing cabinet for a month or six months while you work on other things. Then, when you go back to the article with a fresh eye, you may be able to tweak it, revamp it, and revise it into a salable piece. What is vitally important is that you believe in your work, in your writing. That goes for newcomers to the business and also professionals with decades of experience behind them. Your belief in some of your articles will be tested. Will you give in and be depressed over a rejection, or take a breath and step back up to the plate?

In other words, it's your reaction as the writer that is all-important. Never give up on an article you still believe in, even if a dozen editors have turned it down. Remember that some of the best and most popular works ever published were rejected initially. *The Firm*, by mega-star writer John Grisham, was rejected by thirty publishers. Did he give up? Not on your life. He kept trying, and saw his novel become an international success and a hit movie.

You must decide at the start, if you are a new article writer, that you are going to be a champion at writing and selling articles. That is exactly what the veteran pros have done, and that is why rejection slips mean little to them. They come with the territory. John Grisham and his agent simply moved on to other publishers and finally found one with the vision and good sense to accept *The Firm*. There is a lesson here for all article writers. Editors and book publishers make mistakes; sometimes they are real whoppers.

We say again: Laugh at those rejection slips and move on to your next market. Believe in yourself, consider yourself a winner, and there is no stopping you.

Words of Advice

Here are a few words of advice for writers looking to get published, courtesy of Todd Krieger:

- Do concentrate on the demographic, or audience, that the publication is interested in. Don't pitch a women's mountain biking article to *Road and Track* or an article on cellular telephone services to *Backpacker's* magazine.
- Do exaggerate the magnitude of the story.
- Do submit clips when you are submitting queries.
- Don't miss deadlines.
- Don't miss details when you are on a story and think you will make up for it with colorful writing.
- Don't be shy and afraid of asking the hard questions.

A True Story: The Article That Sold on Its Forty-Ninth Submission

L. P. Wilbur's article about the Mormon Tabernacle Choir was rejected, but the author still believed in it—in spite of an incredible *forty-eight* turndowns. Only one change was made before it went out to market for the forty-ninth time. The article was simply given a fresh title. No other changes were made. The result? It sold. L.P. received a check and acceptance letter.

This should serve as strong proof that faith in your work brings results. Whether you are new in article writing, or a proven professional with many sales behind you, here is a bit of advice: Each time you send a new article to market, make it an intriguing game. Test your psychic power and try to guess which market will buy it and/or which time out will be the magic number. You could even write down your prediction for each article the day you send it out. This can make the entire process much more interesting.

Keep records, keep the faith, and never give up.

Writing Articles
for the Internet

The Internet is an article writer's godsend. It is an incredible world-wide resource that is changing the way writers work, research, play, and earn their income.

Internet consultant Charles Austin sums up the importance of the Internet when he says, "Embrace the Web. It's like an express train—you can either jump on board or it will run you down."

Let's take a look at just a few of the opportunities presented by the Internet:

- It's a research environment unparalleled in modern history—literally a treasure trove of facts, figures, and information about every subject imaginable.

- It's a new medium to sell to. Besides television, no medium has ever sprung up out of left field and captured the public's imagination like the Internet. It's a fantastic business opportunity for writers of all ages.

- It's a twenty-four-hour marketing tool. Post your résumé and some sample articles on a bulletin board, employment Web site, or your own promotional Web site, and writing opportunities will literally fall into your lap. People around the world can hear your voice and sample your writing style, in this wonderful electronic forum.

- And lastly, the majority of information you'll discover online is free! Most writers love reading and the Internet has been referred to as the world's library. The Internet is a powerful research and entertainment tool that no writer should be without.

Selling Your Articles to the Online Market

Let's say you are already sold on the idea that the Internet presents a fantastic career opportunity. And let's further assume you already have access to the Internet (if you don't, we highly recommend you get it). What is the next step a writer should take to sell an article online?

Let's take a moment to examine the sales opportunities. The Internet is comprised of multiple markets that have all converged into the same medium. Book publishing, magazines, the computer gaming industry, academia, retailers, pornography, financial services, Hollywood entertainment, the government, newspapers, health care, directory services, and so on, are all vying for eyeballs—and a piece of market share.

Most of these groups have created Web sites that provide free information to online users. They make their money by charging advertisers to post banner ads on the Web site. Other Web sites, such as *Encyclopædia Britannica*, charge subscription fees for access to their information. Back in 1994, the *Encyclopædia Britannica* migrated to the Internet, and today its Internet information service is making more money online than it ever did in the old days selling its hardcover volumes.

The *Wall Street Journal* is a successful online newspaper that maintains both print and electronic versions of its news and information. Many companies have Internet-only services—content you won't find anywhere in the everyday world. Online-only magazines such as *Slate* and *Suck* have become very popular. These so-called 'zines are simply electronic magazines available via the Internet. There is also the Starwave family of companies. They run sites such as *Mr. Showbiz*, *Outside Online*, and *CyberTimes*, which is the technology section of the *New York Times*.

What do 'zines, online newspapers, and other Internet destinations mean to the writer? We like to call this opportunity. The Internet is a new market to write and sell articles to. There are thousands of Web sites that need fresh content on a monthly, weekly, even daily basis.

Some of the proprietors of these Web sites have little money, so writers' fees are minimal or nonexistent. Other sites are controlled by the same media conglomerates that own the big publishing concerns. They have the money to pay for quality work, with professional creative and editorial staff to add value to stories you might sell them.

So how much money are writers making from selling their online articles? Unfortunately, not too much. Anywhere from 50¢ to a buck a word is standard. High-profile Web sites such as the *New York Times Online* rarely pay more that 50¢ per word.

The key to success in the Internet space is to write and submit articles to only those sites that meet your expectations and interest. Never write solely for the money. If the subject you are writing about does not interest you, that bias will often show up in your work. This is a bad path to follow. A writer's best work must come from the heart. Writing for money alone is a dead-end street. However, if you can find an online destination that truly interests you—say a Web site devoted to technology issues, or children, or an activist site dedicated to saving the white rhino—these are the opportunities to explore with vigor.

Online Queries: Necessity or Waste of Time?

Computer e-mail is a quick way to send an editor a message, and more and more authors are using it. The swiftness of this method makes it appealing, and an author can get a response much faster this way.

"The Internet is especially helpful in the pitching process, when you are thinking about writing a query," says Todd Krieger. "At that point in time you aren't that interested in spending lots of time researching a story that might never run, and the Web can get you the requisite amount of information to form a good query. The Web can be used to verify ideas and facts, specifically those about pop culture, like movies and music. But for the hard stuff—historical, factual, political information—I tend to look to other traditional resources."

Most of the online destinations you target will devote at least one Web page to explaining their submission policy. Our advice: Read and follow the rules. If you want to be part of the team, you've got to demonstrate that you are a team player. Don't believe for a second that "breaking all the rules" will somehow help you stand out from the crowd. That tactic will, of course, get you noticed, but for all the wrong reasons. Silly attention-getting will usually get you blackballed by the Web site, killing future business opportunities.

The query letter has grown considerably in importance in recent years. Many editors of online 'zines and newspapers list a preliminary query letter as a definite requirement for doing business with them. Since most editors have little or no spare time, a strong case can be made for sending a query letter first, whether or not it is an absolute requirement. Editors appreciate this consideration and will be able to get back to you faster because of it.

The advantage of the query letter, for online media as well as for more traditional venues, is that it allows you to sell your article before it's even written. It hits the editor with your basic idea, and if the editor likes the sound of it, he or she will probably want to read more.

A query also gives the editor an idea of your writing style, shows the range of your thoughts about the subject, and provides hints as to whether your basic idea and choice of subject indicate a worthwhile project. A good query letter can convince an editor that you have what it takes to complete an article.

A short (half-page) letter should be enough to describe your article idea, explain why you are an expert in the subject, and why you believe the title would garner interest from a specific group of readers. The longer the query, the less likely it is to be read—especially when submitting via e-mail. Jon Samsel typically sends queries via e-mail that are no longer than two paragraphs in length. Why? That's all it takes to spark the interest of an online editor. A long letter—more than a page or two pages—is guaranteed to take longer to be read and answered. It also tells the editor that you may not understand the Internet writing culture—that less is more. Quick, short, compelling queries are best.

A go-ahead response to a query letter is no guarantee of acceptance. But it does often signal an editor's interest in your idea and possible desire to read an entire article. The best-case scenario, of course, is when an editor commissions you to write your article in advance—working with you to craft an article worthy of that particular online publication. There is nothing like the feeling of writing when you know a check is waiting for you upon completion. It's a true validation of your talent that few writers get a chance to experience on a regular basis. When this happens to you, savor the moment!

If you don't hear back from online editors within two weeks, chances are you won't hear back from them at all. It has been our experience that queries submitted via e-mail are answered pretty quickly—usually within a week or two. Of course, the bigger and more popular a Web site, the longer the response time. If you don't hear anything after a couple of weeks, send another message. Be polite, yet firm in your resolve. Ask if your query was received and when you can expect to hear back from the editor. If you don't get a response to your second e-mail, you could try making a phone call, but this type of rude behavior may be a warning sign. Do you really want to work for a company that can't even respond to its mail? Perhaps it's better to move on, in such instances.

Building Your Digital Writing Portfolio

The reality about writing for the Internet is that few sites can afford to pay much money for the right to publish your material. That's because most sites are not making much money. In fact, most Web sites are not profitable ventures at this time. Even popular Web 'zines like *Wired* are having trouble supporting themselves.

It's no wonder, then, that many Web sites expect writers to work for free. At first glance, this offer may seem totally unacceptable. In fact, it goes against the advice of almost every writing professional we know. The standard mantra is simple—never write for free. And that's a valid statement. But in the online world, the reality is, money is scarce. So what is a writer to do? If you can afford to write for notoriety, exposure, or credit instead of cash, writing for free may be a valid option for you.

For example, if you are a writer with few or no writing credits, accepting two or three free offers to publish your work may be just the thing you need to jump-start your writing career. It is often said that a writer is only as good as his or her last writing credit. Current articles in print can be leveraged in order to land more paying jobs. There is nothing more powerful than phoning an editor and saying, "If you'd like to see samples of my work, you can log online and visit *Wired, Slate,* and *Mr. Showbiz.* I have three articles in print right now online." Since so few writers have their work published online at the present time, getting published on the Internet could give you the competitive advantage you've been looking for to land more work in the traditional print world.

A few writers we know have taken Internet article writing to the next level. They are syndicating their articles to multiple Web sites that have different demographics. Pulling off this scheme is sheer genius, and writers who can syndicate their work on a regular basis can make a lot of money.

How does online syndication work? The syndicator (a.k.a.: the writer) *rents* or *site licenses* the article to an online publisher or portal such as Time-Warner's *Disney*, *Women's Wire*, or perhaps even Ford Motor Company's corporate Web site, for a specific period of time. During this period, the company has the nonexclusive rights to post the article on its Web site. It's a model similar to the one used by traditional press syndicates for popular article writers like Ann Landers and Dave Barry, who write one article that appears simultaneously in regional newspapers and magazines around the world. The writer earns a smaller-than-usual fee per licensed article, but with so many extra buyers, the writer actually earns more money.

Once Published, Take Advantage of Your Newfound Fame

When you write an article and that article is published online, you become known as an expert in the topic, whether you intended to do so or not. That's because the general public looks up to writers—they respect your opinion. As an authority on your topic area, many new and exciting marketing opportunities await you.

For example, article writers can:

- E-mail friends and associates, asking them to read the article, respond to it by submitting letters to the editor, and asking them to let their friends know about the article (if your article is a popular read on a Web site, you may be asked to write another article).

- Teach a class on the subject of your article.

- Write an introduction to an author's book (exposing you and your writing credits to a new audience).

- Contribute ideas to online discussions and cyber-seminars (picking up some extra cash from event organizers while exposing your writing talent to potential buyers).
- Guest host an online chat session sponsored by America Online or CompuServe (again, more exposure for your writing).

As we have mentioned elsewhere in this book, electronic media are becoming increasingly prevalent in our civilization. If you want to be a writer, getting your work on the Web could be one of the wisest moves you will ever make.

Orphan Articles, Filler Articles, and Miscellaneous Writing Venues

You will discover that, much like Freddie in the *Nightmare* series, or Jason in *Halloween*, some of your articles keep coming back. You will look in the mailbox, and see it, again—your SASE, containing that great article you wrote, disfigured by a rejection slip. First, keep in mind that this is normal. Few writers sell 100 percent of their work. It's doubtful anyone can claim that honor.

Orphan Articles

So, what do you do with your orphan articles nobody seems to want? Be resolute: You can and will sell them. Read them over to find out what's wrong. Ask yourself why so many editors are rejecting these particular articles.

Consider these solutions for orphan articles:

- Revise or rewrite them.
- Write a fresh new lead, a stronger ending, and make some changes in the body of the articles.
- Try a brand-new title.

- Add some appropriate quotations in key places.

- Inject some dialogue, if possible, for this can add life to material.

- Try to get a better sense of conflict, setting, or narrative into the work.

- If you first sent out the work with no photos, try including one or more pictures or illustrations. Improving the package in this way may lead to a sale. However, be aware that some unsavory or unorganized editors may return your articles and keep the photos you sent. It happens. Realize that you are sometimes gambling with your photos.

- Approach your subject from a new angle. Then rewrite certain parts of it, and you will find then that it may sell on its next time to market.

This advice from Leon Fletcher, who has seven hundred published articles to his name, should help you fix up your orphans, as well as the rest of your pieces: "Don't let your articles end with whimpers." It makes sense, doesn't it? The ending is the last bit of your writing that the editor or reader has contact with, and you want to make sure it makes an impression. You want people to be left with the feeling that your article is a complete, definitive entity. Take a look at the closing paragraphs of the articles that keep coming back. Are they strong enough? Do they provide a satisfactory conclusion to the story that precedes them? Do they complete or reiterate the main points of the piece? Do they have emotional impact, in keeping with the rest of the article? Rethinking the ending of your article may make it salable.

You'll learn that the articles you write have a will of their own, or so it would seem. Some hit a home run the very first time at bat. Others, the stubborn ones, are picky about where they want to call home; it may take ten or twenty trips to markets before they stop returning. Think of your articles as your children; you want them all to make their way in the world; to be accepted, read, enjoyed, and admired by many people. Some of your articles will be late bloomers, and you will just have to be as patient and as nurturing with them as you would be with your kin.

What else can you do when certain articles keep returning to your mailbox? If you can somehow relate your article to a national event, festival, annual celebration, or historical location, this can help to sell what nobody wanted before.

L. P. Wilbur once wrote an article about Nashville, Tennessee, and the things to do and see there. It kept collecting rejection slips and it looked like nobody wanted it.

What turned things around for that article? While on a business trip to the Nashville area, L.P. discovered a promotional brochure about the Hermitage, the home estate of Andrew Jackson. A tour of President Jackson's home was fascinating. L.P. took notes and procured some excellent photographs. After returning home, L.P. added the information about Jackson's home to the Nashville article. He put together a new package, which contained a cover letter, the rewritten article, and the new photographs. The article sold on its next time out.

When certain articles that you write do not sell after a number of submissions, don't give up. There is usually something you can do to improve their chances: update them, add something fascinating or newsworthy, perhaps get better photos, rewrite the entire piece, perhaps add some examples, or tie it in with some recent or historical event.

When you are able to place your orphan articles—and every honest writer will admit he has some—you will feel more than ever that you have established yourself as an article writer. It's a great feeling, too, to know your orphans have found homes.

Other Venues for Articles

Working in different media can be a useful experience for writers. There may, for example, be periods when your articles don't seem to be selling as well as you would like. At these times, other kinds of writing activity can be used to bring in some quick checks. Let's take a look at them.

PUBLIC RELATIONS WRITING

Business associations and companies often need help with a report, newsletter, or even a feature article. A number of companies produce their own publication, which is distributed to employees, stockholders, and perhaps the general public.

Consider the following possibilities:

- Public relations writing for schools or colleges
- Public relations for politicians
- Public relations for libraries

- Speeches for the owners of small businesses
- Speeches for statewide candidates

ADVERTISING COPYWRITING

Sometimes article writers compose the copy for print ads or radio-television commercials to supplement their income. This type of side-line writing is both lucrative and an interesting temporary change from writing articles.

Author Helen Woodward emphasized one of the strongest truths of advertising: "The best ads aren't the ones about which you say, Isn't that clever? They're the ones that make you take out your money and buy something." Advertising is a selling business. Everything in the industry is geared to moving the product or service for the client.

Like article writing, creating good advertising copy takes a basic ability with words. So the experience you gain in writing articles—the skill of stringing words together—carries over when you write copy for a specific product or service. Copywriters are often called on to come up with concepts, the key phrases or selling ideas that a campaign is built around. Conversely, the talents you polish as a copywriter—the ability to encapuslate concepts, the ability to sell with words—can serve you well when you return to article writing.

Advertising agencies sometimes get behind in turning out new copy, and this is when they look for part-time or freelance help. Radio and television stations and newspapers are also good bets for copywriting work.

After you have a good backlog of articles, it is very possible that any number of them may suggest spin-off ideas for advertising concepts or public relations writing. By reading over your articles, these spin-off ideas may come to mind. In fact, some of your articles may be related to services or products being advertised, so you can take it from there.

There are two ways to land advertising copywriting assignments:

1. Offer your copywriting services to local advertisers in your area. The manager/owners of a variety of small businesses might pay you to help them plan or write the copy for their ads. Using your services would be less expensive for them than using a recognized ad agency.

2. Offer to write copy for near and distant advertising agencies on a freelance basis. You could call on the ad agencies in your city or regional area and let them know of your interest in working with them. Once you have done some actual ad copy work, you will have experience to point to as proof that you can be of help. It would also be wise to get to know some agency copywriters. They might send you freelance assignments when they are pressed for time or just overloaded.

GREETING CARD IDEAS

When L. P. Wilbur first began to write articles, the checks he received for greeting card ideas were a big help. You could also tap this source of extra income while you are gaining skill as an article writer.

Here are some basic facts about greeting cards. You need to be aware of this information before trying to sell card ideas:

- General cards are the traditional four-, eight-, twelve-, or sixteen-line conventional verses you see in the stores.
- Studio cards are those with the funny figures and designs on the front that lead to a clever punch line on the inside.
- Studio cards pay better than general cards.
- Most card companies are currently paying from a hundred fifty to several hundred dollars for the ideas alone.
- Birthday cards are the most popular type of greeting card. Other reasons (subjects) to send cards are get well wishes, wedding, new baby, friendship, vacation wishes, and thank-you.

There are about forty or fifty companies at this time that buy ideas. You can find these markets listed in annual editions of *Writer's Market*, various monthly issues of *Writer's Digest*, and by searching the Internet for companies that produce greeting cards. If you browse the cards in your local stationery store, you will find the publication information printed on the back of the card. Simply write, call, or e-mail the editors of the companies that interest you and request their guidelines for sending in greeting card ideas.

FILLER MONEY

Within the articles you write there are seeds for filler (very short) articles, which is another spin-off type of writing you could do.

Fillers are often only a paragraph or a few lines, from one hundred words or so to several hundred. The demand for these short items is continuous because editors often need them to balance a page or to fill up the small empty spaces of an issue.

Here are some of the filler topics you should try your hand at occasionally:

- Household hints

- Decorating ideas

- Recipes and cooking tips

- How you solved some personal or family problem

- Humorous true stories

- Jokes

- Unusual news items

- Fads, new trends

- Shorts about personalities

- Pet peeves

- Business suggestions

- Short religious or inspirational pieces

- Unusual quotations

Thousands of filler markets are listed in each yearly edition of *Writer's Market*. You are told what kinds of fillers are wanted and how much the publication is currently willing to pay for them.

In truth, filler writing is an excellent way to get started as a professional article writer. Many fillers are nothing but very short articles. If you're a newcomer and don't feel ready to try your hand at a two-thousand word article, why not try the fillers?

Living the Writer's Life

The life of an article writer can be filled with promise and opportunity; but there are some hazards you should know about too.

The freedom of the article writer's way of life is what lures quite a few into the business every year. This basic freedom holds a potential pitfall. You may find yourself postponing what should be done today or this week—research, queries, outlines, or following up on leads. The writer must not put off what he knows needs to be done today. In other words, with freedom comes responsibility.

Resting on your laurels is also a possible pitfall. If you have had a good week or month, it is quite easy to avoid sitting down at your desk. Your mind poses the tempting question, Why not coast awhile? This is a real danger, especially for newer writers.

A third pitfall is uncertainty. The income of a freelance writer can be quite unstable. It's dangerous to assume that you can count on a definite number of sales each month. Until you become an established writer, you must contend with great fluctuations in the earnings provided by your articles.

Actually, this is more of a problem for a full-time writer and, at the beginning, we suggest you keep your day job.

Write Something New Every Day

Unless you are involved with a long article, which can take more of your time, try to write something new every day or, at least, start something. Record the new article ideas that come to you, day after day, and try to find the time to get the best ones launched.

Here is a secret that has worked for many writers over the years: Once you have the beginning done on articles, you are much more likely to finish them. You have time and work invested in articles already undertaken, so it is very likely that you will get them completed and off to market. Those ideas that you can never quite bring yourself to commit to paper may never be finished or see print.

Think about this too. If you wrote a thousand-word article each day of the year, you would have 365 articles. How many of those would sell is anybody's guess, but you would certainly gain experience as a writer, and you would end up with articles to offer. A thousand-word article does not take long to write and consists of about four double-spaced pages. Think about it. What if you sold a third of the 365 articles, or even a quarter of them?

The truth is that honest-to-God article writers never run out of material. If they lived to be five hundred years old, they would still have more articles to write. That is one of the most stimulating and interesting things about being in this business.

Being Your Own Boss

Experienced writers have discovered where they do their best work long ago. If you are generally new to the writing business, then we want to remind you of what was said earlier. As soon as you possibly can, find a regular time and place to write. It doesn't matter if you are working full-time and can only devote a few hours a day to this task; the important thing is to make the commitment.

A regular place lets your mind know that you are serious and that you will be doing your work there every day. Once your mind—especially your deeper, subconscious mind—knows you mean it, it will become your ally and seek to help you. Never doubt this power of your subconscious mind; it can be a great friend for writers.

Some other tips:

- Never go to bed at night without having your work for the next day (preferably for the next week) organized.

- Realize that whatever related aspects of article writing you may like the best, it's the writing process itself—the act of getting words on paper—that results in finished articles and acceptance checks.

- Constantly keep in mind that you are the boss; that you are essentially in business for yourself. Nobody is looking over your shoulder to see that you get your articles written and off to market. It is up to you.

- Reward yourself, now and then. As the boss, you know when you have done your best for a given time period. You will know when you really deserve a day or weekend off. Some writers have a built-in clock that goes off when they need an all-day break.

Little rewards, when you deserve them, will refresh and renew your vigor. Give yourself a day off, go out to dinner at some special place or to an afternoon movie, take a weekend trip, buy something that gives you a lift, or maybe just take a walk or hike for an hour or so. Even a coffee or juice break away from long stints at your desk can clear your head.

A Few Words of Encouragement

This is so important that it bears repeating again: Do all in your power to keep a constant flow of queries on their way to editors, whether by snail mail, fax, e-mail, or telephone. We challenge you to test this for yourself. Get twenty or twenty-five queries off to editors during the next month or few weeks and see what happens. Some will never reply, others may ask for more information or request an outline, still others will reject your ideas, and some unknown number of editors will give you a green light, that go-ahead-and-send-the-article-when-ready response. These numbers will vary or fluctuate, so keep in mind that you can and will improve the results.

You can always improve and rewrite your queries, find a better slant for them, research newer or better information, locate fresher quotes. Just like articles themselves, never give up on pitching ideas you still believe could be effective articles.

As you continue writing, you will discover how the tasks of writing becomes a way of life, and you will enjoy such routine actions as the following (to name a few):

- Reading over old article endings to see if they might be of help in finishing the conclusion or ending of a current article in progress.
- Thinking about new titles, ideas, and subjects at any time of the day or night.
- Alternating periods of longhand and computer or word processor work.
- Thumbing through magazines, newspapers, and newsletters for topics and marketing ideas.
- Starting new articles, if only the first few sentences or the entire lead.
- Worrying if an article you sent six weeks ago has been sent to China, the North Pole, or into oblivion.
- Trying to decipher some of the hurried scribbles done when you were getting too sleepy to write.
- Studying copies of *Writer's Market* year after year, plus monthly issues of *Writer's Digest*.
- Accessing the Internet and browsing online bookstores, such as Amazon.com or barnesandnoble.com, to read writer interviews, reader reviews of books, and to gain knowledge about what's selling and what's not.
- Opening the most promising looking mail first, counting the checks with glee, then tearing up the rejection slips (after laughing at them), filing reply letters, go-aheads from editors, and other correspondence.
- Opening complimentary copies of publications sent to you and seeing your articles in print with your byline.

Always remember that you have everything to gain as an article writer—an all-absorbing new interest, a wide-open shot at any subject of interest to you, an opportunity to build a second or full-time handsome income from your writing, the chance to be your own boss, to live your life with a great degree of freedom, the chance to express yourself directly and write about what you like.

In the appendixes following this chapter, you'll find answers to frequently asked questions about writing and selling articles and several examples of published articles. We'll see you out there in the wonderful world of articles. We wish you the best of luck.

FAQs

Here are some of the most frequently asked questions about writing and selling articles. The answers are offered to encourage and guide you in your life as an article writer.

Once a writer has some published credits, is it easier to sell new material?

Every article must stand on its own merits, whether it was written by an unknown writer or a skilled veteran with twenty years of experience. Published credits do help to get an editor's attention. They also make a writer's byline known.

How many articles does a full-time professional article writer turn out weekly?

Many full-timers try to shoot for four to six articles a day, or more than twenty a week. These would have to be on the short side, or material they can spin off easily. One to three longer articles can usually be done in a day. Other writers spend an entire day on a single article or several days to a number of weeks. If an article requires a series of interviews or extensive research, it will probably take at least a few weeks.

Can several articles be written at the same time?
Many writers have several pieces in the works at all times. It depends on the subject and scope of the articles and how much work they require. One advantage of this method is that when you get stuck on one article, you can turn to the other (or others). It can be stimulating to have several in progress at once.

What other markets exist for articles besides magazines and newspapers?
There are hundreds of syndicates, here and overseas, that buy articles or series of articles from writers. There is also a variety of newsletters appealing to special interests, lots of trade journals that buy, company magazines published for employees, and other special publications.

Would an agent help me sell more articles?
Most agents prefer to handle books because they can make more money. A number of agents handle articles, usually as a courtesy to their book clients. Article writers do not need an agent. You can sell your articles direct to editors.

Does a cover letter have to be sent with every submitted article?
Some writers just send in the article, but it's usually best to include a brief cover letter addressed to the editor who will be considering your article. Some editors view a cover page as protocol. Perhaps, if you have worked a lot with a certain editor, you could simply send a brief note with the article and not a formal cover page.

Does the time when an article arrives in an editor's office have any influence on its acceptance or rejection?
Definitely. Monday is usually a bad time for material to arrive simply because so much other mail arrives. Editors often feel swamped on Mondays. Most magazine editors work three to four months ahead or more. When it's June, they are already working on the September or October issue. Keep in mind also that holiday material should be sent six months early.

How can a writer with some published credits break into the top paying magazines?

By coming up with articles that are so good—so right for the large circulation magazines (or maybe so timely a subject)—that an editor will be eager to snap it up.

Could someone with just an interest in reading be a possible future article writer?

Why not? The potential may certainly be there. Most readers have a real love of words and the many ways in which words can be strung together. Most article writers share this love, but they also have a basic desire to put their own words down on paper, to express their own ideas and opinions. If a reader/potential writer discovers that he has something to say, he will realize this need, and may well put his thoughts into article form.

What advice can you offer on finding the right market for a particular article?

The patience to keep searching for the right market. Form the habit of listing at least four or five likely markets for each article. Do this before completing the article. Many pro writers will not finish an article unless they have five or six good markets for it. Why even start it unless there is good market potential?

Is it better to start with short articles of 1,000 words or with a longer one?

It doesn't really matter, because every magazine has different requirements. Many editors like the 1,000-word article because it fits nicely on one magazine page, accompanied by a suitable illustration or picture.

Does it make any difference where a writer lives?

The answer is no. One of the most attractive features about making money in article writing is the fact that you can do it from virtually anywhere on the map. Article writers are found everywhere and in any number of countries.

Is organizing the material for an article a problem?
Some writers think it is. When they stare at all that research material they have gathered, they feel overwhelmed. From that point, it's a matter of selecting the cream of the crop to use. You become a selector, deciding what to use and what to leave out. You might try the card method. If you do your research on file cards, you will often find it easier to group the cards according to sections of your article. The article can then begin to take shape. Many writers like to research this way.

**Should an article be copyrighted before being sent
to publications?**
No. Publishers won't steal what you send them. Most magazines are copyrighted, and the copyright (covering the articles in an issue) is owned by the publishing company. Editors will inform you (if you ask) as to what rights they are buying. Some magazines buy all rights to an article, while a great many others buy only the first rights.

If you do not wish to sell all rights, you can type "first rights" in the upper right corner of your article manuscript (the first page). Then do not submit that article to publications that buy all rights.

**How long should an article writer wait for a decision before
sending a manuscript to another editor?**
The traditional waiting period used to be a month to six weeks. Because so many more are writing articles today, numerous publications are stating that they take two months to report. A number of new publications are even taking three or four months to respond. Try to deal mainly with markets that will reply within six weeks to two months, which should be long enough to wait.

If no response or decision has been received within six weeks to two months, write a short and polite follow-up letter to the editor. If that is ignored, call them up and keep after them.

**When an editor writes a note on a rejection form or sends
a regular letter—along with the returned article—does this
mean that the writer came close to making a sale?**
The editor in this case probably wants to send some sign of encouragement. If you stay in the field for long (as the veterans know), you will accumulate a lot of nice notes and full-page letters from editors.

I can only spend part of my weekends on article writing.
Would that be enough time to make it worthwhile?
Certainly. Some writers work more slowly than others, but it's entirely realistic for a beginner to produce a few 1,000 word articles each weekend. Over a month's time, even a small weekend production can increase your income and produce a number of published articles.

It's been proven that as little as fifteen minutes of daily writing can produce many finished articles, or even a book, within a year. Even a few hours of writing a week can make you a selling writer.

Can you suggest a market that is not being swamped
with articles?
Most publications that pay a good or fair rate for material and don't hold articles too long are deluged with manuscripts daily. You might try the confession magazines or the fraternal or business magazines with a short article.

Most writers forget about the back-of-the-issue fillers. Make it a point to keep up with a dozen filler markets. Don't forget the tabloids. They buy a lot of fillers, and some of them pay handsomely for article ideas.

Sample Articles

Some Tips Toward More Effective Practice

BY MIKE MYERS

This article was first published in Modern Drummer *(July 1988). Reprinted by permission.*

At one time or another, we've all heard that ageless expression: "Practice makes perfect." But does it really? If so, why do some drummers practice almost endlessly, only to achieve limited results, while others practice a minimum amount of time and advance rapidly?

Setting aside natural-born musical abilities, the answer lies in individual practice methods. There are almost as many different practice meth-

ods as there are drummers. Some practice routines are conducive to improvement, while others actually restrict it. Practicing just for the sake of practicing cannot ensure progress, and neither can poorly organized occasional practice.

Since practice methods vary significantly from person to person, it would be difficult, if not impossible, to prescribe a "correct" way to practice. However, there are some successful practice methods that I have observed and also recommended as a teacher, which bear offering in an attempt to make your practice time more beneficial.

1. Locate a practice space. The first procedure should be the location of a suitable practice facility. Where it is situated is not really important. (I have practiced in bedrooms, bandhalls, practice rooms, and even a storage closet in an unused corner or a church.) The important thing is to make sure that the area has adequate lighting and ventilation, and can be securely locked. Places where equipment can be left for extended periods of time usually work best.

Next, check with everyone within earshot of your practice area. Make sure it is okay with them if you practice, and agree on what hours of the day it will be tolerated. A method I always use is to approach neighbors, friends, etc., explain that I am going to be practicing drums nearby, and promise not to practice past 10:00 P.M. I also ask them to call if the practicing ever becomes too loud. (So far, no one ever has.)

2. Plan practice sessions in advance. Planning is one of the most crucial elements of effective practice. An enormous amount of practice time is often wasted due to poor planning and organization. A person who boasts of practicing an hour a day may in fact be wasting as much as thirty minutes sorting through materials and deciding what to work on, or playing over material that is already mastered. Know what you want to accomplish before each practice session. Simply going in to the drums thinking that you will become better just because you are practicing anything won't do.

3. Long-range/short-range goals. Plan long-range as well as short-range goals.

Long-range goals are self-set goals for six months or a year from now, such as "I want to be able to play a good samba groove." Short-range goals are for today, like "I am going to learn samba exercises 1 to 10 on page 30." Map out beforehand realistic/obtainable long-range and short-range practice goals, and set out to achieve them.

4. Set up a specific practice order. If a specific practice order is followed from day to day, practice time will become more beneficial. The key is to make the best use of available time in order to produce the maximum results. Having a specific practice order that is regularly followed gives an organizational structure to practice and leaves less to chance. This is not to say that you may not want to vary your order from time to time, in order to give extra attention to a certain area. But planning a regular daily practice routine will be a step in the direction of more effective practice. Here are my suggestions, along with a possible time allotment for each.

a. Warm up (five to thirty minutes)

Warm hands up by practicing rolls, technical exercises, scales, rudiments, etc. This prepares the hands, as well as the mind, for challenging material ahead. Be cautious, though, not to practice technique exercises blindly with no thought processes involved. Careful thought and evaluation should be given to technique each day, in order for improvement to take place.

b. Learn new music/correct problem spots (thirty minutes to one hour)

At this time, the mind and hands are the most alert. Use this time to learn new music and correct problem spots in old music. You can use this time for working out that fill-in during the bridge of the song that you folded on at the job last night, cleaning up the two seven-stroke rolls that are always sloppy, learning the notes of the run on the third page of the mallet solo, getting the tuning changes worked out that take place between movements of the timpani solo, etc. Have specific goals in mind that are determined before beginning to practice.

Many times, this is the most frustrating segment of practicing. It is often difficult to work on new or challenging music. But remember, Rome wasn't built in a day, and neither was Gadd. Miracles can't happen overnight, so be realistic. Don't attempt too much in one practice. Take big problems and break them down into a bunch of small problems, then convert them into your short-range goals, and attack them one at a time. It is much better to take a difficult measure and practice it again and again

until played perfectly, than to stop every time that measure is encountered and say, "I always have trouble with this part."

c. Take a break (five minutes)

During practice sessions longer than an hour, take a short break. After an intense practice, you will need one! Let the mind relax a bit and refresh for what is ahead. After a break, the mind is clearer and can function more efficiently. Long practice sessions go more smoothly if interspersed with regular short breaks.

d. Review learned material (ten minutes to one hour)

Go back and play the piece that you have been correcting all the way through. Then, if desired, play other material that brings you personal pleasure. This can be music you learned last week or last month. The whole purpose of this practice segment is to reinforce concepts you've already learned.

e. Sight-read (ten to thirty minutes)

Somewhere in the latter part of the practice session, it is a good idea to sharpen an important musical ability—the art of sight-reading. The sight-reading potential is often the most underdeveloped musical ability we possess. It needs constant practice and refinement. Daily sight-reading practice will be very beneficial.

Make sure to locate good literature to practice sight-reading. Don't choose material that is too difficult; it may become discouraging and also will not carry over to actual situations. On the other hand, don't read music that is too easy, or the skill will not carry over to situations where actual sight-reading is required.

5. Conclusion of practice. When concluding practice sessions, some people like to do physical exercises—as well as other playing exercises—which they call "warming down." Other people turn immediately to the television. I like to reflect back over the session, and think about what I accomplished and where I still have to go. I will think about such things as: "The four problem measures at letter A are going much better today; I'm finally playing the correct rhythm in the last two measures; I'm understanding the song form much better now."

While everything is still fresh, plan short-range goals for tomorrow, such as, "I'm playing better fills on the rock chart, but tomorrow I will improve my time and polish the fills a bit more," or "Tomorrow I'm going to work out the second phrase at letter C that I didn't get today," etc. It's better to work out your goals when you have a chance to realistically monitor your progress.

6. Daily schedule. Every teacher recommends a different practice schedule. Some require seven days a week, while others may only require two or three. I personally recommend practicing a minimum of five days a week. You will find that the greatest progress will occur when you plan an individual practice schedule and stick with it, week after week. It will become a routine—part of your life!

Again, I must state that there are many good practice methods. I have only presented one approach, which has proven successful for myself and my students. Take some time, and concentrate on which method will work best for you. Then, plan out a personal practice schedule to produce the maximum results.

Raising the Bar: 9 Ways to Improve a Business-to-Business Web Site

BY JON SAMSEL and LAURIE WINDHAM

This article was first published in e-business *magazine (July 1998). Reprinted by permission.*

Ken Orton didn't set out to revolutionize the e-commerce travel market. In fact, what he initially set out to do was transform a TV-based travel programming company into a networked online travel business. What Orton and team managed to do in the process is shake up the $101-billion U.S. travel agency market—growing their company into one of the most comprehensive, easy-to-use, and enjoyable travel destinations on the Internet. Preview Travel is now a mega-travel information and transaction site—with over 220,000 cumulative customers and 3.4 million registered users. Preview Travel's innovative Web tactics exemplify what's expected of next-generation, e-commerce Web sites.

The question executive managers should ask themselves is not a new one—"How can I re-tool my Web site so that it becomes more productive and engaging for my users?"

A Productive Web Site

Business-to-business Web sites must enable users to perform their jobs better. Productive Web sites have a depth and breadth of content. The one thing today's Web visitors will not tolerate is unwanted marketing material "pushed on them" over the Web. Users will "click away" when they sense they are being "sold."

The site must hold their attention, empower them, and cause them to want to come back. This is engagement—and it's not an easy technique to master.

Nine Principles for Improving a Web Site's Effectiveness

The following nine principles may improve the effectiveness of your business-to-business Web site:

1. Know Your Audience

Today's most productive and engaging Web sites understand their audiences. Businesses can learn more about their visitors by asking questions such as:

- Who are your users, and why do they come to the site?
- How experienced are they with your technology, services, and/or products?
- What type of content do they come back for and what might compel them to come back more often?
- Is localization important—what language choice do they need?
- Do they want peer-group interaction?

- How long does it take for them to find what they need, and how can you improve this experience?
- What functions and features do they really need?
- What are their purchasing preferences relative to your products/services?

These questions can help shape the productivity and functionality of a Web experience. For example, businesses need to know where their Web site visitors are in the cycle of consuming their products, as well as how those visitors define productivity.

What's productive to a prospect is different than what is productive to a customer. For the prospect, Web productivity means easy access to purchase information, pricing, product specifications, comparative analysis, and basic company data. A customer's view might include easy access to tech support, software patches, chat rooms, and FAQs.

Using research techniques like focus groups to identify common user attitudes or commissioning formative usability tests to discover what areas of your site are most effective can arm you with critical data needed for e-commerce success

2. *Identify Topline Content Objectives*

Today, innovative technology companies are developing new Web services at a blistering pace. But deploying new Web content doesn't always achieve the desired results. Content managers frequently jump into production mode without first identifying the objective(s) of their sites relative to the consumption cycle.

Define your main goals and establish clear objectives to create a solid foundation from which to build an efficient and engaging experience.

3. *Leverage Existing Content*

Online content can originate from traditional sources: catalogs, data sheets, press releases, advertisements. Sometimes content creators can repurpose this material in new and innovative ways, but some content that was first intended for print does not translate well to the online world.

Web visitors have an uncanny ability to spot sales and marketing material disguised as "new" Web content. They don't like to be fooled. Just because you can repurpose content doesn't always mean you should.

One way around this problem is to integrate your marketing and mixed-media campaigns creating a cross-media solution. In the past, content creators from different departments within the same company created their own assets that solved their own unique needs (commercials, print ads, brochures, radio spots, stationery, etc.). Now content creators can build digital assets that can be distributed or "shared" from one department to all departments. Your strategic message is "authored" or "branded" once and incorporated into many mediums throughout many departments—both traditional (print, direct marketing, video) and electronic (Web, Intranet, CD-ROM, e-mail, kiosk).

4. Build Dynamic Environments
Businesses need to create unique ways to express their content within the confines of the digital screen. Unique content is more than superior graphic design. It's a Whole Experience that engages the visitor with both content and functionality. The experience is the message.

Business-to-business sites can take a page from successful consumer Web sites such as Amazon.com, which is pioneering next-generation customer satisfaction with collaborative filtering technology like BookMatcher.

Dynamic online environments allow the visitor to give feedback on how to improve the product or ser-

vice offered by the company, or allow visitors to communicate with other users with similar interests. Web managers can also create "self-service" applications that empower customers, employees, vendors, and partners to interact with the content they need most.

Database delivery of customized content can also bring Web pages to life. One thing is for certain: current generation Web sites—with their static content, poor integration, and inferior interfaces—lack personalization and won't be good enough for long.

5. Create A "Whole Structure" Access System
The Whole Experience Web site should satisfy the visitor's needs, pull visitors through the Consumption Cycle, and accomplish this task by providing the quickest, most efficient path between any two locations within the site.

This access methodology must be planned—a collaboration between the technologist, writer, and designer. This special team must think as one—a strange amalgam of architecture, storytelling, and design—to create a Whole Experience that works.

As content increases, the underlying structure of a Web site can become quite complex. Taking a Whole Structure approach, rather than simply a "page display system," means going beyond the typical organizational system to a "matrix of distributed solutions"—a dynamic solution for both company and customer.

Whole Structures are systems which:

- Promote intelligent navigation
- Offer quick and efficient search capabilities
- Ensure that unique/personalized content needs are met
- Empower visitors to discover their own solutions

- Promote "ease of transition" through the Consumption Cycle

6. Test the Interface
The media displayed on a computer screen should be compelling and interactive, whenever possible.

Designed properly, the interface helps prospects and customers successfully navigate the site. Designed poorly, the interface interferes with a user's goals and objectives.

Interface design is an area that can benefit from professional usability research because it must account for everything a user can, might, and will interact with. Everything from sight, sound, and touch must be meticulously planned and implemented in order to achieve the optimum end-user experience. The most powerful interface designs are those which seamlessly meld navigational tools with graphic images. The right mix creates a unique identity—an atmosphere, theme, and access methodology for your business-to-business Web site.

7. *Unify Vision, Style, and Theme*
Follow the rules of good graphical design:

- Try not to crowd your screen with too much content
- Use fonts that are pleasing to the eye
- Use white space (yes, less is sometimes better)
- Stick with a specific color scheme
- Design for the screen with a sense of balance
- Use images instead of text whenever possible (one image speaks louder than a chunk of words)
- Implement universal concepts that visitors will be able to relate to in an emotionally engaging way
- Use symbolism to represent abstract concepts (when appropriate)

Make sure your brand and corporate vision shine through

the site, but do it subtly. Try not to hit the user over the head with blatant marketing propaganda.

8. *Write for the Web*
First off, let's state the obvious—writing engaging content for the Web is no simple task—especially for content creators who come from traditional disciplines such as advertising, marketing, journalism, customer support, technical documentation, or copy editing. Writing for the Web requires a deep understanding of the concept of interactivity—and how interactive multimedia experiences engage more than one sense to stimulate the user.

It is the Web writer's task to help the content-planning team create both a functional and dynamic site that combines page layout, multimedia content, interactivity, network tools, commerce, and human interface design. Writers must play a more complex role than simply copy-fitting for the screen. They need to become techno-savvy and start "thinking like designers and programmers" in order to gain the insight needed to effectively create for the electronic mediums.

9. Give Something Back

One of the key functions of a business-oriented Web site is gathering visitor demographics. Businesses lure users onto their sites to "officially register" their products and seem surprised when their requests are met with stiff opposition. We sometimes forget that we in the United States live in a culture that vigorously protects its privacy. Users are hesitant to provide personal information over the Internet without first receiving assurances that the business will not sell their names to third-party marketers. Businesses need to respect and reward participants.

Interestingly, recent studies have found that many Web site visitors are willing to participate in online registration if it will help personalize their online experience. The personalization is the reward. This also applies to any application that, in return for information, empowers the customer to make their own decisions and take immediate action to get what they need.

Today's businesses face the exciting challenge of transforming their first- and second-generation Web sites into dynamic end-user experiences that are more productive and engaging for people at all points of the consumption cycle. For businesses whose bottom line depends on reaching prospects and customers via the Web, engaging and productive content is the solution.

The Law of Karma: Believers Claim We're Charting Our Future Right Now

BY L. P. WILBUR

This article was first published in the Watchman Expositor *(November 1987). Reprinted by permission.*

Believers in reincarnation tell of the law of Karma and describe it as an unchangeable rule of the universe. Whatever a soul in any one lifetime sows—that soul will reap the same in a future life.

In other words, there's no escape. If you were one who helped throw Christians to the lions in the days of Nero (in Rome), you'll have to pay for this in some future life. Thus, sooner or later everyone pays his or her karmic debts. The good or evil we do returns to us in our own futures.

The whole idea of this Law of Karma is summed up in the title of an old hit record by Kay Starr: "Wheel of Fortune." Each new lifetime affects how this wheel will turn for us in the future.

We are then creating our own destiny—through each of our individual karmas.

But to accept the Law of Karma is to believe that each of us returns to earth again and again—whether we want to or not.

Some say they would prefer total destruction, a nothingness after death rather than coming back. Others cling to the Christian ideal of an eternal Heaven. But the Law of Karma gives no choice in the matter. The lessons we fail to learn, the growth we did not attain, the good or harm we did, all influence the conditions of our future lives.

We cannot stop this karmic law from working, say the believers in reincarnation. As an example of karmic justice, they'll claim

Hitler will have to pay for what he did in the 20th century. Who knows how long or how many hard lifetimes will be needed before his karmic debt is paid. Ages, no doubt!

Most of those you talk to about reincarnation, from all walks of life, either believe in it or reject the entire idea. Through the centuries, many have believed in the rebirth cycle with firm conviction, but it has never attained universal popularity.

Of course millions will believe in whatever they want to believe. Nothing can change their minds. In the day of Columbus, the vast majority refused to put any stock in the notion that the world was round.

Even today, in our modern society, there's an organization still devoted to the belief that our planet is flat. Despite all the overwhelming evidence to the contrary, they won't change their beliefs.

True or not, there's something appealing about the thought of getting another chance, and a third, fourth, fifth, and so on. If you strike out a few times, there's no worry; you'll have many more times at bat—many more lifetimes.

Such an idea of hope is irresistible for many people. It appears to them to be a new, a different kind of hope, as opposed to the traditional ones they've studied and heard preached so much before. And firm believers in reincarnation will even cite scripture references to support their idea.

Reincarnation and Karma are fascinating to speculate about. But, as with many people, my own dislike for the idea of returning to earth keeps me from being a believer. I frankly object to the idea of being re-educated over and over in future lifetimes. To my way of thinking, that's backtracking. And I think God moves forward—not backward!

Whatever our beliefs in what lies beyond the wall of death, most ethical and religious systems are so set up that there is encouragement to live a good life on earth right now. That is one point in which the Law of Karma and traditional Judeo-Christian beliefs are in agreement: somewhere, in another life on earth, in the hereafter, or right now, both the pain and the joy you cause will be returned to you. Think about it!

The Six Most Common Barriers to Developing an Effective Web Business Strategy

BY JON SAMSEL and LAURIE WINDHAM

This article was based on a two-hour business presentation. CIO Magazine *requested that the presentation be condensed into a 350-word article for publication.* Published in CIO Magazine *(April 1999)*

When it comes to leveraging the Web as a critical business vehicle, companies are realizing that the biggest obstacle to success is themselves. The challenge for executive management today is how to overcome internal resistance to the inevitability of the Web. Based on thousands of hours of Cognitiative's "Voice of the Customer" research and studies we've conducted with a range of large companies, we've identified six common barriers business leaders face as they take on the challenge of defining and deploying a Web business strategy: (1) Knowledge of what customers want, (2) Existing business strategies and practices, (3) Leadership, organizational structures, and funding models, (4) Existing skill sets, (5) Technology solutions, and (6) Internationalization.

Let's probe the first two barriers a little deeper.

Knowledge of What Customers Want

Addressing the needs of online constituents in a fulfilling and differentiated way requires a deep understanding of them. We suggest approaching this as if you were developing a new product—define your market requirements, survey the market and competitive landscape, talk to your target constituents; find out what business partners want; test the usability of the site experience; and track satisfaction. The key is to understand why people come to your Web site and what actions they take when they are there so that you can develop a proactive site strategy that satisfies their needs. And be aware—this process never really stops. Keep a constant pulse on your efforts because Web-savvy customers are increasingly demanding.

Existing Business Strategies and Practices

Resolving conflict with existing business strategies is another critical barrier to doing business on the Internet. This can run the whole gamut from pricing, product development, logistics, channels, required investments, and how customers are served. An interesting exercise is to construct a hypothetical Web strategy for your market as if you were a start-up company. What would your business model be? Where would you invest? How might a competitor invade your space? Addressing these issues can help drive clarity on the required business strategy.

Dare to Always Have a Dream

Change Your Life for the Better with
These Words of Wisdom

BY L. P. WILBUR

First published in Complete Woman *magazine (December 1991)*

You've heard of vitamin power, money and political power, and so on, but have you ever thought about dream power and what it can do to change your life for the better?

Millions of women discover, sooner or later, that even the security of a job, career, or profession isn't enough.

A dream can change that empty feeling, fill you with renewed vigor, and give you an ongoing reason for making the most of your time on earth.

What a Dream Can Do For You

Here are just a few of the advantages of having a dream in your life:

- A dream gives you a purpose, a reason for being, an objective.
- A dream stimulates your imagination and creativity.
- A dream keeps you more enthused about life in general.
- A dream motivates you to think ahead and plan for your future.
- Having a dream you're determined to fulfill can keep you more healthy. Medical experts have proven that boredom can actually kill you. A dream keeps you alive and humming on all cylinders.
- A dream enables you to get much more out of life in the way of personal satisfaction.
- A dream provides you with more overall zest for living.

Some Dreamers and the Dreams They Attained

There's an old saying that "brown eyes belong to dreamers." It's true, but the eyes of dreamers are also blue, hazel, green, and what have you! Anyone can dream, and millions do, but the great majority, unfortunately, let their dreams die too soon. They reason that the odds are too great against them realizing their dreams. So what happens? They give up much too soon; they throw in the towel and admit defeat.

People like this who give up too soon on their dreams possibly never heard about the remark once made by General George S. Patton when a British general told him that a military move Patton already had underway "was impossible." Patton merely smiled at the general and replied that "the impossible is what we're in business for."

Others also fanned the flames of their dreams. As a little girl, Marilyn Monroe stared out a window and dreamed of being on the silver screen some day. Through a series of small parts, she built a steadily rising name and film image. In *The Prince and the Showgirl*, Marilyn proved that she had considerable acting talent. Though she died far too early, she left her footprints in a place of honor and did make her dream a reality.

Ben Hogan, a fine golf professional, thought he would never play the game again after a bus hit his car head-on in a terrible accident. But Hogan's dream still burned brightly He had already been a golf star for years, and he didn't like being forced out of the game that he loved—especially through no fault of his own.

Even though his doctors said that his golfing days were over, Hogan kept fanning the flame of his dream. He resumed playing the game. Difficult as it was, he kept at it. The happy result was that

Hogan became a champion all over again—a champion for the second time around.

Dolly Parton wanted to be a singer and songwriter. She learned the ropes in Nashville, built a name for herself, and enjoyed a number of hit records. But Dolly's dream had a vaster horizon. She reached out for more, and in recent years, her career has broadened in other directions, with Las Vegas, films, and television using her talent.

How Do You Get Dream Power Going for You?
Here are some proven guidelines for launching a dream of your own and making it become a reality:

- If you don't now have a dream you would like to see come true, decide on what your major want, goal, or objective is. What is it that would make you very happy and bring you lasting fulfillment? You must try to come to grips with what it is, although most people, certainly the majority, are well aware of what their dreams are.
- Write out a clear statement or description of your dream.
- Start thinking about your dream a lot and develop an intense desire to achieve it.
- Formulate a plan or series of steps you can take toward the fulfillment of your dream.
- Work or move toward attaining the first step of your plan.
- When you reach one step or goal of your plan, begin at once to head for the next one.
- Remember each day that most people succeed by taking a lot of little steps. Keep your eyes on one step or goal at a time and do all you can to get to that place in your plan. Once you arrive there, then you can set your sights on the next destination point of your plan.

- Whenever you come across any item, idea, bit of advice, suggestion, guideline, pointer, or whatever that might help you move closer to your dream, write it down and try to use it, or make it a part of your plan. Over a period of years, you'll discover and learn a lot of things that will help you make your dreams come true.
- Visualize yourself as already having your dream. See yourself with the dream you want fulfilled, think how happy it will make you feel, and simply act like you've already realized it. This is pretending of course, but there is definite power in acting this way. This is the very way a great many have gotten the things they want and made their dreams (at least some of them) come true.

Stay on Course
Toward Your Dream

You must keep everlastingly at it. You have to try to move closer every week to your dream and do something, preferably every day, to help bring the day of fulfillment nearer.

Studying the careers and lives of others who attained their dreams can be of definite help to you. When people you know, or hear about, achieve their dreams, try to discover how they went about accomplishing it. What were the sacrifices, the strategic plans, if any, the stepping-stones, and the overall coordination in their cases? There are clues to be found in the study of how various achievers have reached their dreams. What worked for them may well work for you too.

Dreams Do Come True

Finally, write these words in blazing red letters across the screen of your mind and in the central core of your being: Dreams do come true. Many people all over the world have experienced the unique thrill of realizing one or more important dreams in their lives. I see no reason why you cannot do the same.

But to achieve what you want, you must know what your dream is, build a very strong desire to achieve it, work out a sensible plan for the steps or series of goals leading to your dream, and then apply your plan relent-lessly (plus updated, stream-lined versions of your plan), regardless of the obstacles you may see in your pathway.

I'll be betting on you and believing that you can and will make that dream in your heart a tangible reality. May you know that joyous moment of a dream fulfilled. There's nothing else quite like it. More power to you!

The Power of Praising Employees

Motivating People with the Positive

BY L. P. WILBUR

First published in Piedmont Airlines *magazine* (*July 1986*).

Most companies now realize that some employees will work harder and more productively for praise than for money. The wise manager knows, of course, that a good salary is important, but money is no longer all that counts today. The majority of workers expect more now. Praise for good work completed, or in progress, has become increasingly significant to them.

A local branch manager for an insurance company took an active and continuous interest not just in each agent's sales production, but in each person as an individual. There was never any doubt that he was pleased with the hard work and good results of the sales team. He believed in praising people whenever they deserved it.

How did he praise them? Not only did he list the effective producers each month on the assembly-room blackboard; he also saw that each agent who merited it was recognized at the weekly sales meetings. And he let each one know personally how he felt by praising him in front of other office staff members, as well as in his own office during various meetings with employees.

Why praise workers and employees? One strong and basic reason is fulfillment. Everyone likes to feel that he or she is *appreciated* and that the quality of his work is noted and pleases his manager and company. The days when an employee worked for money alone are just about gone. Most workers of today fully expect to be recognized for their consistently good job performance. True, there are still plenty of workers who are mainly motivated by money, but the best ones, the employees who really put down roots and make a real contribution to their firms and companies over a period of years, are usually those who received a healthy amount of praise for their good work. They thus found job fulfillment and interest, so they stayed with the company.

The question of why employees should be praised really gets down to the old cliché that "a company is often known and judged by the way it treats its employee." There are, of course, a lot of companies across the country that do not praise employees: The word gets around, and such companies that refuse to recognize worthy workers usually have a fairly high rate of turnover. Some employees will even admit that they switched companies several times, in order to find one that treated its employees fairly.

Praise is a definite form of acceptance. With all the problems and confusion of today's modern living, more and more people from all walks of life seek the assurance of knowing they are *accepted* and *approved* by others. Such acceptance can be as vital as food is to our bodies.

It is true in many cases that a man or woman who does not receive praise at home will look for it elsewhere. And some of us crave praise much more than others.

Keep in mind that something often happens in people when others express belief, acceptance, and approval of them. Pierre and Marie Curie believed in each other and eventually discovered radium. Grace Kahn believed strongly in the musical ability of her husband Gus. This praise and confidence paid off big. Gus Kahn wrote a long string of remarkable song hits like "It Had to Be You" and "I'll See You in My Dreams."

Breathes there an effective manager who does not use motivation every day? Actually, another form of motivation is praise. Certainly the right and enthusiastic use of praise can definitely motivate employees to higher levels of quality work production. Tests now show that various kinds of plants do respond to warm words of praise by growing much faster. As a manager of people, try to keep in mind that praise is one of the 25 dominant human wants or desires. Just about everyone wants to be praised by others. Keeping this in the forefront of your mind will help you not to miss any chances to praise employees who deserve it. Those you manage will appreciate your recognition and could well develop into some of your most valuable employees.

Even proven employees, who have done good work for a number of years, need to be praised occasionally at least. Anyone can sometimes be engulfed by a feeling of depression, commonly known as the blues. The horror of the blues can turn an otherwise efficient employee into someone walking around in a daze. Your words of praise might come at just the right time when said employee *needs* to hear something positive. P. T. Barnum, the brilliant promoter and showman of the last century, warned that anyone seeking success should avoid becoming a victim of "the horror of the blues." Winston Churchill called the blues "the black dog." Praise fights the blues and can send them packing.

One of the big pluses of a career on the lecture circuit is praise. Professional public speakers and actors, as well, all enjoy the praise they receive for their work. The applause and praise of their audiences and fans mean far more to some performers than the money they earn. Famous singer Al Jolson insisted on being able to see the faces of his audience when he sang. The delight and approval registered in their faces was a tonic to Jolson. It meant everything to him.

Praise does a lot to form a positive attitude. According to Clement Stone, the Chicago business tycoon, a positive mental attitude (PMA) is vital to success: "Self-development. Do it now. Direct your thoughts, control your emotions, ordain your destiny. Dare to aim high. Keep your mind on the things you want and off the things you don't want. Positive mental attitude—I feel healthy, I feel happy, I feel terrific." Every time you praise your employees and workers, you are helping them to form and maintain a PMA.

Here are some suggestions for using more praise in your daily contact with employees.

- Praise those you manage whenever they deserve it.
- Look for reasons to offer words of praise and be alert for any and every opportunity to recognize a worker who has performed his or her work with quality, dedication, and cooperation.
- Watch for any chances to praise employees in front of others and during staff meetings.
- Spoken praise of an employee or worker may also be followed up with a note or letter of commendation.
- When worthy and useful ideas are offered by employees, be certain that they receive praise for them. Some companies offer cash rewards, along with such praise.

Do not forget this dynamic word. It has only six letters, but these letters spell out an open sesame way to tap more effective and productive management. Praise is a tried and proved method that really works. It can lift a worker from the lower ranks of a company and transform him or her into a valued key employee.

The type of management that includes plenty of praise in its policy will be a more harmonious and successful one. Your employees will remember it and will give their all for a manager who appreciates them . . . and lets them know it.

Those Magic Referrals

BY L. P. WILBUR

This article was first published in Truck Sales and Leasing *(April 1991).*

There is no better time to ask for referred leads than right after wrapping up a truck or lease sale. Your prospect has been converted into a customer, and possibly a friend. His or her confidence in you as a sales professional, and in your goods and/or services, is running high. This is the ideal moment to request referred leads—those magic names that can lead you to additional sales and profits.

To savvy salespeople, making a sale is not the end of a process, but an important step to continued sales success. They view the closed sale as the resource for a network of new sales through referred leads. They ask the customer for the names of others who might be interested in their products and services. To skip this step, say these salespeople, is like throwing away money you find in your pocket.

At the point when you have made a sale, your buyer will more than likely be happy to refer business to you. These referred leads—be it the name of an individual, company, or organization—should be treated as valuable information. Those in the same type of business are in a good position to know of other prospects with similar needs and problems.

Some who acquire truck leases from you will give you referred leads but may not wish for you to use their names. These leads are commonly called "cold names." It is always best to get the customer's permission to mention his name. The value of the referral is enhanced when you can drop a name when contacting the lead.

When a stranger knows that you have been recommended by a friend, neighbor, or business associate, the reception you receive often is warmer and friendlier. You will gain more immediate acceptance from the prospect, as well as diminish the chances of a quick refusal.

Pre-Screening

Referred leads are not your only source of new truck/lease prospects. However, they are one of the very best. Some of the leads you receive will prove to be duds. But by qualifying the leads before contacting them, you can find yourself on a more direct trail to those who will buy from you.

Successful sales pros offer the following suggestions for gaining referred leads:

- Ask questions to trigger the mind of the person giving you the leads. For example, "Do you know someone who needs a truck, uses a truck in their work, or who may have mentioned they are in the market for a truck?"

- Get as many facts about the leads as possible—type of business, current equipment, transportation requirements, present needs, etc. This will save time and help you spot the hotter prospects.

- Always record the information you are given. Make sure you have the correct spelling of names and the proper titles of company officials.

- Always get permission to mention your customer's name when contacting the referred lead.

- Contact the referred leads right away while the information and impressions are fresh.

- Always express your appreciation to those customers who refer business to you. By all means, report back to them on your results.

As a final suggestion, the veterans recommend sending prospects to your customers or supplying them with leads. This is an effective way to develop an ongoing relationship, they say. It is natural for a person to respond favorably to you when you show your appreciation and helpfulness.

Remember, once a sale is made, your job is not completed. The next step is to get some referred leads. Do not skip this important follow-through step. If you do, you are in effect walking away from additional truck/lease sales. Referred leads are a rich source of additional sales.

How to Write a Classified Ad

There's an Art to This Brief Pitch

BY L. P. WILBUR

This article was first published in Income Opportunities *(September 1992).*

Starting your own business means nothing unless you have customers to buy your product or service. Often, depending on what type of business you have, placing classified ads in the right newspapers and periodicals can bring those customers.

So sharpen your pencil and get out some paper. Make yourself comfortable, but keep your thinking cap on tight. You're about to write a classified ad, starting from just a single word or a headline.

This could be a helpful exercise for you, especially if you continue to practice writing classified ads on your own. You're going to discover how much fun there is in creating a classified ad. But finding the best way to sell a product or offer is also a real challenge.

Creatively speaking, it's stimulating to work up an attractive classified ad. But again, remember that what you want is not to entertain the prospect or to show how clever you can be with words. Your only goal must be to choose and use the strongest selling words. You want words that will make prospects send you an order at once.

Choose a Magnetic Headline

Here are some brief pointers about headlines in general. Try to remember them whenever you're looking for a strong opening line.

1. A catchy headline is memorable.
2. The best headlines are usually short. Never have too many words in the opening line.

3. Prospects want to know what a product will do for them.

A headline can often sum up the benefit to the customer most effectively. Let's assume, just for example, that you've developed a manual or booklet to sell by mail. It's an $8.95 booklet that would have strong appeal for women looking for an executive position and to other women seeking to reenter the job market. You wish to sell the booklet directly from an ad.

With a booklet as your product, how would you write a classified ad to sell it? What would you use as a headline? Jot down any ideas that come to mind right now.

If your objective is to get prospects to request more details, you can often do it in a very few words. If your goal is to sell something directly from the ad, it will take more words.

To stimulate your thinking, here are some examples of mail-order headlines. They are taken from a variety of classified ads:

- IDENTIFICATION CARD SALES KIT!
- HOW TO BORROW UP TO $25,000 WITHOUT INTEREST!
- HOW TO START A RESUME WRITING BUSINESS IN YOUR SPARE TIME!
- MAIL-ORDER MILLIONAIRE HELPS BEGINNERS MAKE $500 WEEKLY!
- NEW LUXURY CAR WITHOUT COST!
- MONTHLY AS PUBLISHER'S AGENT!

Now let's match headlines for the booklet geared for those women who are looking for an executive position. The headline should command attention and offer your prospects the promise of value for their money. Here are several examples that would be strong openers:

- WOMEN—HOW TO LAND THAT EXECUTIVE JOB

- LAND AN EXECUTIVE JOB—
  WHATEVER YOUR AGE
- WEALTH AND STATUS CAN BE
  YOURS TOO!

Remember, your goal in writing a headline is to get across the promise of what you're offering as quickly as possible. Prospects want to know what's in it for them, and what it will do for them. How does your own headline compare with the three suggested above? Maybe you did much better than you think.

Do you believe any of the three headlines above would grab a woman's attention, as she scanned a mail-order classified ad section? Certainly those women who are interested in a career—and there are millions of them—would want to read beyond these headlines to find out more about the offer.

Ask yourself if your own headlines would grab the attention of women and make them want to know more about your offer. You may

have come up with several strong headlines for the booklet. If so, try to choose the one you feel would do the best selling job. You could, of course, run several ads with different headlines for the booklet. If you were just trying one ad at first, however, which of your headlines would you select?

When some of the ads you run don't bring the results you want, you might try switching the headline. Sometimes a change in the headline can improve the pulling performance of an ad.

Describe the Product

The next step in our ad for the booklet is to describe the product or service you are offering. In other words, let your prospects know what the product or service will do for them. The headline of our ad has implied the promise of the product or service, so now make the nature of it clear. Is what you're offering a home study course, a device, a service, or a novelty item?

The second line in our ad might be something like this:

NEW BOOKLET TELLS HOW

A variation of this second line could be:
PROVEN PLAN REVEALS SYSTEM.

If you used "proven plan," it wouldn't make it as clear to prospects that the product being offered is a booklet. So it would be wiser to substitute the word "booklet" in place of "plan."

Now we have two lines for our booklet ad. Using the second headline, these lines are:

LAND AN EXECUTIVE JOB—
WHATEVER YOUR AGE!
New booklet tells how.

The price of the product or offer usually comes next, along with some type of guarantee. There are several ways this could be stated in our booklet ad. Here are some of them:

- ONLY $8.95—GUARANTEED!
- RUSH $8.95 (GUARANTEED) CASH OR MONEY ORDER TO . . .
- $8.95—ONE MONTH GUARANTEE!

If you wish to have a time limit on a guarantee, you might want to state it in the ad, as the third line above does. If the guarantee is ten days or two weeks, you should say so.

Call for Action
Next is a call for desired action. Without an appeal to prospects to take action by sending you an order at once, an ad would be stripped of one of its essential elements. Make it a definite rule from the start in your business to always appeal for *immediate* action.

This action appeal in our ad could be any of the following lines:

- ORDER TODAY!! STERLING ENTERPRISES, (KEY AND ADDRESS OF COMPANY)

- WRITE, MORRISON COMPANY, (KEY AND ADDRESS)
- ACT NOW!! (COMPANY NAME. ADDRESS, AND KEY)

Now let's put all of these lines together to make our total booklet ad:

LAND AN EXECUTIVE JOB— WHATEVER YOUR AGE! New booklet tells how. Only $8.95 guaranteed! Order today!! Sterling Enterprises, 789 Oak St., Dept. PS4, Miami, FL 39871.

There's our completed booklet. "PS4" stands for the April issue (4 meaning the fourth month) of *Popular Science* magazine.

The total number of words is twenty-five (twenty-four if the zip code is allowed free). Notice the exclamation marks in the ad. Use them to give an added effect to the total ad and to make it longer when published. The use of "street" or "avenue" was also omitted in order to save one word.

Now let's create a second ad for this same booklet. This time, however, we'll use a different headline, description, and appeal:

WEALTH AND STATUS CAN BE YOURS TOO!! Proven booklet reveals system. Rush $8.95 (guaranteed) cash or money order to: Sterling Enterprises, 789 Oak St., SSI, Miami, FL 39871.

It's perfectly alright for you to try selling a product both directly from an ad and also by the inquiry-and-follow-up method. Once you learn which selling method pulls the best for a given product or service, you can stick with that choice. Some products priced over $5 sell fairly well directly from an ad. You'll have to test specific products and prices. As a general rule, however, items sold directly from an ad will do better if kept low priced.

The point is to not get discouraged if an ad does

poorly. If the price you're asking seems too high (over ten dollars), you might just get prospects to send you requests for details by running small ads like you see in many magazines, and then following up with sales literature. Of course, you would then need a sales letter to send back to the prospects to persuade them to send you an order.

It's a good idea to actually write several different ads for each product or offer that you plan to advertise. You'll gain some excellent experience by creating small classified ads, and your chances of coming up with a strong ad will be improved.

Never believe that any particular ad you write is the best you can do. The more ads you create, the better you'll become at it. Copywriting is a developed skill; it improves with time and practice.

Good luck and may the classified ads you write and run fill your mail-box with many orders.

The "Groundhog Day" Phenomenon: A Lesson in Customer Convenience

BY JON SAMSEL

This article was first published in Bottom Up—The Magazine for the High Tech Start-up *(May 1999).*

If we can assume that online customers demand something more from a company doing business on the Web, why is it then that so many companies put so little effort into getting to know what their online customers need? What's so hard about identifying a user, listening to what they have to say about conducting transactions online, and delivering an online experience that meets those expectations?

Two words explain this phenomenon—power shift. Most companies still placate their customers, rather than treating them like business partners. That's understandable. Businesses are not used to interacting with consumers any other way. But technology has empowered customers to interact with the company across many mediums in ways

they have always wanted to. This shift in power from companies making decisions about what's best for a customer to customers demanding that role for themselves makes a Web-sited transaction much different from the same experience which occurs in a off-line world. Older venues push, sell, or haggle to preserve some control over the customer's impulses, questions, or anxieties. In a connected economy, businesses respond to customers' desire for information, then, "enable" rather than "control" the eventual transaction of goods or services.

This doesn't mean that companies like Intel need to dismantle its manufacturing plants, or Barnes and Noble its bookstores. It does mean they need to respond to customer's desires to also have access to products and services on the Web. Consumers do show strong preferences for conducting certain transactions—like buying books or computer equipment—or conducting other business such as procuring office products, paying bills, trading securities, or booking travel tickets—electronically, rather than in person or over the telephone. Electronic commerce enables individuals to do what they want, when they want to. It makes things convenient.

Convenience seems to be a consistently underrated commodity. One reason that very sophisticated businesses have underestimated the appeal of the Web is that they have not taken into account the value of convenience. Consumers who prefer online transactions do so largely because it takes less effort and less time than do alternative venues. And as the Web evolves it will become even more user-friendly, al-

lowing consumers to spend their time even more efficiently than will older systems.

In the 1993 feature film comedy *Groundhog Day*, Bill Murray plays a reporter named Phil Connors who travels to small-town America—a place called Punxsutawney, Pa.,—to do a story on the infamous Punxsutawney Phil, an overweight groundhog who every year informs the nation whether or not spring will arrive early. Connors reports on the story and somehow manages to survive the day. But something strange happens during the night. Upon awakening the next morning, he discovers that it's Groundhog Day all over again. It seems he's trapped in some kind of time warp where he's forced to relive the same day over and over. Each day, the townspeople greet Connors as if he were a stranger, even though the man spent time chatting and interacting with them the previous day. The redundant, interpersonal exchanges aggravate Connors to no end—turning him into a frustrated, angry, and suicidal man.

Many of today's business are doing the same things to their customers—they treat them like strangers. This only serves to alienate, frustrate, and inconvenience them.

Let's take this real-world story, for example. Our tale begins with a woman who walks into a bank and tells the account manager she'd like to take out a loan. The manager asks the woman to fill out a loan application, a legal-sized piece of paper that takes her fifteen minutes to complete. Even though the woman has been a customer at the bank for over ten years and all her personal information is on file already, the woman has no choice but to complete a loan application. The woman is then told that the bank will call her once it's had a chance to review her loan request. The manager and the woman shake hands and the woman leaves.

But instead of waiting for the bank to call, the woman decides to log onto an online banking service and complete an electronic loan application that takes her only two minutes to complete. The Web-based loan service doesn't ask the woman to fill out a giant form because it has developed a database system that talks to all the various credit agencies simultaneously and completes the missing data fields automatically so the woman doesn't have to. With little or no effort, the Web-based service has just provided the woman with more personalized customer service than the bank that supposedly has a ten-year relationship with her. Seconds after submitting her online request, the woman receives a reply—her $10,000 loan has been approved at a 9.8 percent annual interest rate for a 24-month term. Monthly payments on the loan are $485. The woman verifies the loan request with a mouse click and the money is wired into her bank account within two days.

One week later, the woman gets a call from her regular bank. "I'm happy to inform you," offers the cheery loan manager, "that your loan has been approved."

The woman replies rather dramatically, "I'm happy to inform you that you're no longer my bank."

This good-humored anecdote is meant to drive home an important point. As the Web decentralizes brick-and-mortar industries such as insurance, financial services, travel, and real estate—in addition to many aspects of sales, marketing, manufacturing, and distribution—businesses must adapt to the growing expectations of their customers if they hope to keep them. The Web has changed what people expect from an insurance company, travel agency, real estate agent, technology vendor, and bank. The Web impacts all suppliers of goods and services by giving consumers tools for accessing information on product and pricing which used to remain in the provider's folded hands. Customers now expect to interact on an equal footing with these providers. A buyer is now empowered in ways she has never been before and it puts her in a position of leverage over those who provide goods and services. Consumers can now demand that businesses treat them more like partners, rather than pawns in a rigid, inflexible system.

In *Groundhog Day*, Bill Murray's character vents his frustration in a way which mirrors customers stuck doing business with companies who still don't "get" the Web. "What would you do," Connors asks, "if you were stuck in one place and every day was exactly the same, and nothing that you did mattered?" It's a quote from a movie, but it could easily be attributed to a frustrated bank customer, a novice home buyer, an angry computer purchaser, or a bitter insurance shopper. The Groundhog Day phenomenon—treating customers the same old way, day after day—is a losing proposition. Businesses who insist on managing their patrons and prospects in this manner will risk losing the one commodity they've always counted on—consumers without choices.

Suggested Reading List

Burgett, Gordon. *Sell and Resell Your Magazine Articles*. Cincinnati, Ohio: Writer's Digest Books, 1997.

Hennessy, Brendan. *Writing Feature Articles: A Practical Guide to Markets and Methods*. New York: Focal Press, 1997.

Holmes, Marjorie. *Writing Articles from the Heart: How to Write and Sell Your Life Experiences*. Cincinnati, Ohio: Writer's Digest Books, 1993.

Jacobi, Peter P. *The Magazine Article: How to Think It, Plan It, Write It*. Bloomington, Indiana: Indiana University Press, 1997.

McLarn, Jack Clinton. *Writing Part-Time—For Fun and Money*. Wilmington, Delaware: Enterprise Publishing Company, 1978.

Shaw, Eva. *Writing and Selling Magazine Articles*. Washington, D.C.: Marlowe and Company, 1995.

Sloan Wray, Cheryl. *Writing for Magazines: A Beginner's Guide*. Chicago: NTC Publishing Goup, 1997.

Sova, Dawn B. *How to Write Articles for Newspapers and Magazines*. New York: MacMillan General Reference, 1998.

Wells, Gordon. *The Craft of Writing Articles*. London: Allison and Busby, 1997.

Serials

1999 Writer's Market: Where and How to Sell What You Write. Kirsten Holm, ed., 1999 edition. Cincinnati, Ohio: Writer's Digest Books. (Also available on CD-ROM.)

Writer's Guide to Book Editors, Publishers, and Literary Agents. Jeff Herman, ed., 1999–2000 edition. Rocklin, Calif.: Prima Publishing.

The American Directory of Writer's Guidelines. John C. Mutchler, ed. American West Books. (June 1997)

Poet's Market. Chantelle Bentley and Tara A. Horton, eds., 1999 edition. Cincinnati, Ohio: Writer's Digest Books.

International Literary Marketplace. 1998 edition. New Providence, N.J.: R.R. Bowker.

Christian Writers' Market Guide. Sally Stuart, ed., 1998 edition. Harold Shaw Publications.

Editor and Publisher Market Guide 1999 (75th Edition). Ian E. Anderson, ed. New York: Editor and Publisher Co.

Index

A

academic article, 15
acceptance, article, 115, 116, 148
    effect of published credits on, 147
acceptance, query, 132
advertising copywriting, 140–141
advice, as idea source, 53
agents
    celebrity, 16, 105
    use of, for sales, 148
airline magazines, as market, 18
Allen, Steve, 47
all rights, 150
Amazon.com, 146
"America Means More to Me Than
    My Job" (article), 77
America Online, 135
Amtrak, 7
anecdote, 90–92, 98, 138
    defined, 90
    finding, 91–92
    guidelines for, 92
    as idea source, 91
appointments, interview, 105
article
    defined, 11, 13
    focus of, 11–12
    goal of, 11
    length of, 144, 149, 151. See also
        filler articles, as market
    samples of, 153–194
    structure of. See structure, article
    types of, 13, 44
*Artists and Writers International
    Book*, 124
art-of-living article, 15
assignment work, 132–133
    advantages of, 19
    for family articles, 19
    interviews, as source for, 105
    outlines requested before, 64
    and payment, 64, 115–116
"Atlantic Theater Company: Evolving
    Structure" (article), 62–63
Austin, Charles, 32, 129
authority, establishing
    with online articles, 134–135
    with use of facts, 94–96, 99
    See also credibility, establishing
Author's Guild (N.Y.), 37
autobiographical essays, as idea
    source, 8

B

Bach, Marcus, 23
Barber, John H., 82
barnesandnoble.com, 146
Barry, Dave, 8, 134
belief, as idea source, 52
books
    as anecdote source, 91
    as idea source, 36

Bridges of Madison County, The, 16, 62
burnout, as subject, 22. *See also*
    depression, as subject
business article, 25–27, 98
    idea sources for, 35, 37, 142.
        See also ideas, sources for
business magazines, as market, 151
business manager, celebrity, 16, 105
bus magazines, as market, 18
byline, 2, 146, 147

C
California Highway, 12
card method, for research, 150
Carton, Sydney, 96–97
case histories, use of, 94. *See also*
    examples, use of
celebrities, as idea source, 54, 55, 142
celebrity article, 16–17, 55
    anecdotes, in, 90–91
    idea sources for, 35, 51, 56, 142.
        See also ideas, sources for
    interviews for, 105, 106, 107.
        See also interviews
change, as idea source, 56
children, as idea source, 8
circulation, publication, 2–3, 4, 9
civic event, as idea source, 49–50
civic events article. *See* current events
    article
clichés, as idea source, 83
clichés, use of, 55, 83
Clinton, Hillary, 8
clip file. *See* idea folder
closing paragraph, 84, 138, 146
"Coca-Cola: The Soft Drink That
    Changed the World" (article),
    60, 99–101
command
    as idea source, 54
    as paragraph lead, 75, 77
commercials, writing. *See* advertising
    copywriting
commissioned work. *See* assignment work
comparison, use of, 75, 96–97
comparison lead, 75

competition, industry, 109, 110, 134,
    149. *See also* sales, article
CompuServe, 135
computer
    query, by, 116, 131–133
    submissions by, 115, 121
    word processing software for, 42, 45
    as writing tool, 41–42, 45
computer article, 23–24
    idea sources for, 35. *See also* ideas,
        sources for. *See also* high tech
        article; technical article
confession magazines, as market, 151
"Confidence in Yourself Is Money in
    the Bank" (article), 77
contacts, use of, 16, 26–27
contrast, use of, 86, 96–97
contrast lead, 75, 83
cooking tips, as filler topic, 142
Cool, Lisa Collier, 120
"Coping with Customer Skepticism"
    (article), 60
copyright, 69, 71, 150. *See also* rights,
    publication
copywriting, advertising, 140–141
Corbett, Jim, 54
cover letter, for submissions, 148
Crater of Diamonds (article), 30–31
credibility, establishing
    with use of facts, 99
    use of interviews for, 103, 107.
        See also authority, establishing
credits, published, 147, 149
curiosity, as idea source, 56
current events, as idea source, 56
current events article, 14, 19–20
    idea sources for, 35, 49–50, 56, 57,
        138, 139. *See also* ideas, sources for
CyberTimes, 130

D
danger, as idea source, 50
"Dare to Always Have a Dream:
    Change Your Life for the Better
    with These Words of Wisdom"
    (article), 171–175

dashes, use of, 86
Davis, Patti, 54
declarative statement, as idea source, 52
definition lead, 75
depression, as subject, 15. *See also*
     burnout, as subject
dialogue, as lead style, 75
Dixon, Jeanne, 16
Dragon Naturally Speaking
     (software), 42
dramatic lead, 74
dramatic phrase, as idea source, 53
dream, as idea source, 56
"dummy" title, 70

E
"Earth's D Day, The" (article), 69
Eastwood, Clint, 16
e-business (online magazine), 24
editor
     article acceptance by, 115, 132, 148
     and article changes, 110, 114–115
     and article titles, 68, 69, 70, 115
     of foreign publication, 123
     online, 132
     and publication schedules, 148
     and query replies, 115, 116–117, 132
     rejections by, 125, 150. *See also*
          rejections
     research on, 44, 112
     response time, 116–117, 150
     retaining photos, 138
     submission format for, 114, 115.
          See also publisher guidelines
     traits of, 109–111, 115
Einhorn, Richard, 63–64
electronic magazines. *See* online
     magazines
Ellison, Larry, 51
e-mail, use of
     for queries, 116, 131–133
     for submissions, 115, 121
emotion, as idea source, 50
emotional response, from readers, 90
Encyclopædia Britannica, 130
ending, article. *See* closing paragraph

entertainment article. *See* celebrity
     article
Entertainment Weekly, 106
environmental article, idea sources
     for, 14, 36
essays (autobiographical), as idea
     source, 8
event, as idea source, 49–50
everyday objects, as idea source,
     56–57
exaggeration, use of, 126
examples, use of, 93–94, 102
Excite (search engine), 107
eyewitness interviews, 5

F
fact, as idea source, 49
facts, verifying, 131
fair use, 96
family article, 19, 142
     idea sources for, 35. *See also* ideas,
          sources for. *See also* inspirational
          article
FAQs, 147–151
fax, use of, 115, 121, 124
feeling, as idea source, 50
fees. *See* payment
Feldman, Ruth Duskin, 19, 21
"57 Ways to Sell a Pickle" (article), 62
file cards, use of, 150
filler articles, as market, 141–142, 151
films, as idea source, 38
Firm, The, 125–126
first paragraph. *See* lead paragraph
first rights, 113, 150
fitness article. *See* health and fitness
     article
Five *W*s (article structure), 59–63, 73
flashback lead, 74, 76
Fletcher, Leon, 138
floppy disk, use of, 115, 121
focus, article, 11–12
     as rejection reason, 12–13
folder, idea, 33–34
food, as subject. *See* health and fitness
     article

foreign markets. *See* overseas markets,
    sales to
fraternal magazines, as market, 151
Frumkes, Roy, 107
Fryxell, David, 20
future events, as, 14, 56

G
Gardner, John, 110
Gates, Bill, 83
Gehrig, Lou, 95
general interest article, 14–15
    idea sources for, 34. *See also* ideas,
    sources for
Globe, 17. *See also* tabloids, as market
government agency publications,
    as idea source, 36
graphics, use of, 97–98
"Great Love Can Change Lives, A"
    (article), 93
greeting card ideas, writing, 141
Grisham, John, 125–126
"'Groundhog Day' Phenomenon:
    A Lesson in Customer
    Convenience, The" (article),
    86–87, 190–194
Gunther, Max, 89

H
happiness, as subject, 14
hardworking paragraph, 86, 87
Hayes, Ira, 73–74
health and fitness article, 21–22
    idea sources for, 34, 35, 53–54, 56,
    142. *See also* ideas, sources for.
    See also self-help article
Hemingway, Ernest, 47
Hewlett-Packard, 24
high tech article, 23–24. *See also*
    computer article; technical article
historical event, as subject, 139
historical figures, as idea source, 54
hobby, as idea source, 55
holidays, as idea source, 6, 51, 138, 148
Holmes, Marjorie, 13
hotel publications, as market, 18
"house style", publisher, 115

"How Do You Face Crucial
    Moments?" (article), 61
how-to article, 18, 20–21
    idea sources for, 52, 54–55. *See also*
    self-help article
"How to Write a Classified Ad"
    (article), 184–189
*How to Write Articles for Newspapers and
    Magazines*, 15
How To Write Irresistible Query Letters,
    120
Hugo, Victor, 47
human interest, as lead style, 73–74
human interest article. *See* inspirational
    article
humorous articles, 15, 142
humorous encounters, as idea source,
    54
humorous lead, 75
Hunt, John, 33
hyperlink, 31, 33

I
idea folder, 33–34
ideas, article, 12–13, 18, 144
    as spin-offs to other ideas, 27, 33,
    140, 147
    testing of, 113–114
ideas, sources for, 5–9, 29–31
    idea folder, as, 33–34
    Internet, as, 31–33
    interviews, as, 104
    list of, 34–39, 49–57. *See also*
    specific article types
illustrations, use of, 97–98. *See also*
    examples, use of
income, writing, 41, 143. *See also*
    payment
inflight article. *See* airline magazines,
    as market; travel article
influencing people, as subject, 52
informational lead, 75, 78, 82, 86
Infoseek (search engine), 107
inspirational article, 23, 32–33
    idea sources for, 51, 142
    sample title for, 69. *See also* family
    article; religious article

international markets. *See* overseas markets, sales to
Internet, 129–130, 146
 and access fees, 45
 advantages of, to writers, 129–130, 146
 as greeting card company source, 141
 hyperlinks on, 31, 33
 as idea source, 31–33
 as publisher guidelines source, 113
 as research tool, 24, 107
 as sales market, 2. *See also* online sales
 search engines, 107
 use of, for fact-checking, 131
 use of, for marketing, 129–130. *See also* Web site
Internet article. *See* computer article
interviews, 103–108
 advantages of, 103–105
 effect on writing time, 147
 eyewitness, 5
 how to conduct, 105–107
 as idea source, 7, 8–9
 multiple, 106
 and "off the record" comments, 106
 practice exercises for, 108
 props for, 107
 as research source, 5
 tape recording of, 43–44, 105, 106, 107
 by telephone, 17
 tips for, 27
 and transcript edits, 106
 use of contacts for, 16
introductory paragraph. *See* lead paragraph

J
Jackson, Andrew, 139
Jong, Erica, xii
journal, writing, 39, 53, 54
journals, 38
 as idea source, 37

K
Kelton, Nancy Davidoff, 13, 15
"kill fees," 116

Krantz, Judith, 47
Krieger, Todd, 29, 98, 126, 131
Kroc, Ray, 96

L
Landers, Ann, 134
Laughton, Charles, 30
"Law of Karma: Believers Claim We're Charting Our Future Right Now, The" (article), 166–168
lead paragraph, 73–80
 defined, 73
 exaggeration in, 76, 79
 function of, 73, 84
 practice exercises for, 79–80
 samples of, 59–60, 62, 76–78, 82–83
 tips for writing, 18, 25, 75–79
 types of, 73–75
 word selection in, 76, 79
 writing of, for motivation, 144
libraries, as research tool, 111, 130
lifestyle choice, writing as, 2, 143, 146
 advantages of, 2–4, 9
 factors in choosing, 3–4
 working hours for, 3
list method, 86–87. *See also* outline, article
local events article. *See* current events article
location, as lead style, 75
location, writing. *See* office location

M
magazines
 as idea source, 34–36
 obtaining samples of, 112
 online, 24, 130, 133. *See also* journals
managers, celebrity, 16, 105
marketing
 with published credits, 147, 149
 use of Internet for, 2, 129
markets, sales, 148, 151
 advertising copywriting, as, 140–141
 filler articles, as, 141–142
 greeting cards, as, 141
 identifying, 34, 111–113, 123, 126, 149

online, 2, 129, 130–131
public relations writing, as, 139–140
syndicates, as, 148
tabloids, as, 17
writing for specific, 112, 126.
    See also specific article types
Mavis Beacon Teaches Typing
    (software), 42
McDonald's, 96
McKinney, Don, 18, 31, 34
medical article. *See* academic article;
    health and fitness article
mental health, as subject. *See* health
    and fitness article
Merrill, John, 5
metaphors, use of, 83, 85
Michener, James, 47
Microsoft Network (article), 51, 83
Microsoft Word (software), 42, 45
midsection, article, 89–102
    elements of, 89–90, 102. *See also*
        specific elements
    function of, 84
    goal of, 89
    guidelines for, 102
    practice exercises for, 102
    summary samples of, 98–101
midsection, paragraph, 82
money, as subject, 14
"Money Making Entrepreneurs"
    (article), 59–60
Montaigne, Michel de, 8
mood, as idea source, 50
Mormon Tabernacle Choir (article), 126
motion pictures, as idea source, 38
Mr. Showbiz (online magazine), 130
Murray, Donald, 21
museums, as idea source, 37
musical event, as idea source, 49–50
music article, 12
    idea sources for, 35. *See also* ideas,
        sources for. *See also* current events
        article

N
National Enquirer, 17. *See also* tabloids,
    as market

national event article. *See* current
    events article
nature article. *See* environmental
    article, idea sources for
newsletters, 91
    as idea source, 36–37
    as market. *See* public relations
        writing
newspapers, 91
    as idea source, 30–31, 34, 51, 54
    online, 130, 131
*New Standard Dictionary of the English
    Language*, 11
"New Success Secrets" (article), 85
New York Times, the, 54, 130
New York Times Online, 131
nonexclusive rights, 134
notes, interview, 106
numbers, use of, 94–95, 102
nutrition article. *See* health and fitness
    article

O
obituary, as idea source, 51
observation, as idea source, 50
office equipment, 42–45. *See also*
    computer
office location, 43, 144, 149
    change in, for inspiration, 79
office supplies, 42–44
"off the record" comments, 106
"Of Mice and Me" (article), 76
O'Hara, John, 43
onetime rights, 113
online journals, as idea source, 37
online magazines, 24, 130, 133
online newspapers, 130, 131
online sales, 2, 129–135
    establishing authority with,
        134–135
    markets for, 2, 129, 130–131
    payment for, 131, 133, 133–134
    query letters for, 131–133
    and site licenses, 134
    and syndication, 134
online syndication, 134
opening paragraph. *See* lead paragraph

organization, article, 150. *See also* outline, article

orphan articles, 137–142

Orton, Ken. *See* Preview Travel (article)

outline, article, 63–64, 115

    included in query letter, 117–118

    and list method, 86–87

Outside Online, 130

overseas markets, sales to, 113, 122–124, 148

P

paragraph, hardworking, 86, 87

paragraph structure, 81–83, 88. *See also* structure, article

parenting article. *See* family article

parsing method, 65–66

Passion of Joan of Arc, The, 63–64

patriotism, as idea source, 55, 77–78

Patton, George S., 90–91, 93, 172

payment, 133–134

    on acceptance versus publication, 116

    for assignment versus unsolicited work, 64, 116

    and editor-requested rewrites, 115

    factors affecting, 2, 5

    fluctuations in, 143

    by foreign versus domestic publication, 122, 123

    for greeting card ideas, 141

    as lifestyle reward, 2

    for online sales, 131, 133

    reference source for, 44. *See also* income, writing

People magazine, 106

personal experience, as idea source, 38–39, 52

personal manager, celebrity, 16, 105

philosophical statement, as lead style, 75

photo archive, 97

photographs, use of, 2, 97–98, 138

    for interviews, 107

    and sources for, 97, 104

physical condition, as subject, 53–54. *See also* health and fitness article

poem lead, 75

political events article. *See* current events article

political scandals, as subject, 122

postal service, use of. *See* "snail mail"

"Power of Praising Employees, The" (article), 176–180

prayer, as subject, 23

Premiere magazine, 106

Preview Travel (article), 82, 159

printer, computer, 42, 45

problem, as idea source, 18, 52, 142

professions, as idea source, 56

profile article, celebrity. *See* celebrity article

promotion. *See* marketing

"Pros and Cons of Keeping a Supervision Diary" (article), 77

publications

    circulation of, 2–3, 4, 9

    as idea source, 36

    obtaining samples of, 112

    and Web sites for, 4

public relations writing, 139–140, 148

public speakers, as idea source, 37

published clips, use of, 118–119, 126

published credits, 147, 149

publisher guidelines, 118

    and "house style," 115

    importance of knowing, 64

    sources for, 112–113

publishers, and use of artwork, 98. *See also* photographs, use of

publisher schedule, 148

Q

query, 64

    editor replies to, 115, 116–117, 132

    published clips included with, 118–119, 126

    response time for, 110, 116–117

    by telephone, 110

    tips for, 22

    unsolicited, 116

    use of, versus submission, 118. *See also* submission, article

use of SASE for, 116. *See also* query
    letters
query letters, 116–120
    advantages of, 132
    defined, 117
    multiple, 116, 121, 145
    online, 131–133
    publisher guidelines for, 118.
        See also publisher guidelines
    rewrites of, 119, 145
    samples of, 119–120
    tips for, 117–118. *See also* query
question
    as idea source, 51
    as lead style, 74, 77, 78
    as paragraph transition, 85, 87
"Question of Honor, A" (article), 78, 99
Quinlan, Anna, 8
quotation, use of, 95–96, 102, 138, 142
    and misquotes, 106
    as paragraph transition, 85, 87
quotation lead, 75, 78, 83

R
"Raising the Bar: 9 Principles for
    Improving a Business-to-Business
    Web Site" (article), 24, 159–165
Random House Dictionary, 11
readers, and how articles help, 3, 4, 9,
    23, 24, 25
Reader's Digest, 54, 92, 99
Reader's Guide to Periodic Literature, 118
Reagan, Ronald, 54
received wisdom, as idea source, 53
recipes, as filler topic, 142
recreational vehicle publications,
    as market, 18
"red book". *See Artists and Writers
    International Book*
"Referred Method, The" (article), 77
rejections, 114, 124–127, 150
    and article focus, as reason for, 12–13
    factors affecting, 148
    and rewrites, 125, 137, 139.
        See also orphan articles
relationship article, family. *See* family
    article

religious article, 23
    idea sources for, 35, 52, 56, 142.
        See also ideas, sources for. *See also*
        inspirational article
rent, article. *See* site license, article
repetitive phrase, as paragraph
    transition, 85, 87
reprint rights, 113
research, article, 5–6, 19
    card method, for, 150
    effect on writing time, 147
    Internet, as tool for, 24, 31, 129, 131
    and interviewee, as source for, 104
resort publications, as market, 18
response time, editor, 116–117, 150
rewrites
    as additional sales source, 26, 27, 112
    after article rejection, 125, 137, 139
    of queries, 119, 145
    requested by editor, 115
    of titles, 70, 72, 115, 137
rights, publication, 44, 113, 134, 150
    and copyright, 69, 71, 150
    reference source for, 44
routine, writing. *See* schedule, writing
"Rudeness on the Road" (article), 12

S
sales, article
    and agents, 148
    effect of foreign sales on, 123
    effect of titles on, 67, 71, 72
    effect on, with photos, 98, 138, 139
    online. *See* online sales
    to overseas markets, 113, 122–124,
        148
    from rewrites, 26, 27, 112
    tips for, 111–113
sample articles, 153–194
sample reports, use of, 96, 102
Samsel, Jon
    and e-mail queries, 132
    and idea sources, 31, 51
    and list method, 86–87
    and technology article, 24
    and travel article, 18

SASE (self-addressed, stamped
    envelope), 114, 123
    and "snail mail," 115, 116, 121
scene description, as lead style, 75
schedule, publisher, 148
schedule, writing, 3–4, 45–46, 143,
    147, 151
    and parsing method, 65–66.
    See also work methods
school event, as idea source, 49–50
school events article. *See* current
    events article
Schultz, Bob, 17
science article
    idea sources for, 35, 37–38. *See also*
    academic article; technical article
search engines (Internet), 107
season, as idea source, 50. *See also*
    holidays, as idea source
second paragraph (article structure), 25
    function of, 84
    sample, 61
second rights, 113
"Self-Employment Picture, The"
    (article), 78, 86
self-help article, 24–25
    idea sources for, 36, 56. *See also*
    ideas, sources for. *See also* how-to
    article
shared trait, as idea source, 53
"Sharpen Your Competitive Edge"
    (article), 78
Sherman, Allan, 99
shocking lead, 75, 77–78
shocking phrase, as idea source, 53
sidebars, use of, 97–98
site license, article, 134
"Six Most Common Barriers to
    Developing an Effective Web
    Business Strategy, The" (article),
    169–170
Slate (online magazine), 130
"snail mail," 115, 116, 121
    and SASE, use of, 114, 123
software, word processing, 42, 45
"Some Tips Toward More Effective
    Practice" (article), 153–158

Somewhere in Time, 61
Souter, Gavin, 98–99
Sova, Dawn B., 15, 20
special journals, as idea source, 37
speechwriting, 140
spin-offs, idea, 27, 33, 140, 147
spiritual article
    idea sources for, 52, 55. *See also*
    inspirational article; religious
    article
sports article
    idea sources for, 35, 49–50, 56
    and interviews, 106. *See also*
    interviews. *See also* current events
    article; health and fitness article
sports event, as idea source, 49–50
Star, The, 17. *See also* tabloids,
    as market
"Start-ups versus Start-agains: the
    Battle of the Net Economy"
    (article), 8–9
Starwave, 130
statistical information, as idea source,
    52
statistical lead, 74
statistics, use of, 94–95, 102
stock photography agencies, 97
structure, article, 87
    elements of, 84. *See also specific
    elements*
    Five *W*s, in, 59–63, 73
    guidelines for, 84, 86–87
    outline for, 63–64. *See also* outline,
    article and paragraph transitions,
    85–86, 87
structure, paragraph, 81–83
    guidelines for, 82
    midsection, in, 82
    practice exercises for, 88
subheads, use of, 102
subject, article, 12, 22. *See also* ideas,
    sources for
submission, article, 64, 113–121
    and assignment work, 64, 115–116.
    See also assignment work
    competition in, 109, 110, 134, 149
    cover letter for, 148

and editor, 109–111, 113–116, 150.
See also editor
effect of published credits on, 147
identifying markets for, 34,
111–113. *See also* markets, sales
and original manuscript, 114
to overseas markets, 113, 122–124
and publisher guidelines, 64,
112–113, 115, 118, 121
rejections of, 124–127. *See also*
rejections
response time for, 150
unsolicited, 64, 115, 116, 118
use of, versus query, 118. *See also*
query
use of SASE for, 114
success, as subject, 14
Suck (online magazine), 130
Sullivan, John L., 54
"Sydney: Saturday City" (article)
syndicates, as market, 148
syndication, article, 9, 134

T
tabloids, as market, 17, 151
Tale of Two Cities, A, 96–97
tape recording, 42, 107
of interviews, 43–44, 105, 106, 107
and transcript edits, 106
"tearsheets". *See* published clips, use of
technical article, 15–16
idea sources for, 37–38. *See also*
ideas, sources for. *See also*
computer article; high tech article
telephone, use of, 105
to contact editor, 110, 115, 117, 133
for interviews, 17
telephone recording. *See* tape recording
television, as idea source, 34
"Ten Ways to Get More from Your
Time" (article), 25
third paragraph (article structure), 61
"Those Magic Referrals" (article),
181–183
time, as subject, 25
title, article, 67–72
changes to, 68, 70, 72, 115, 137

and copyright, 69, 71
"dummy" title for, 70
as idea source, 55, 70
kinds of, 71
practice exercises for, 72
as step in defining article focus, 12
tips for creating, 68–69, 71–72
train magazines, as market, 18
train rides, as idea source, 7
transcriber, 42
transitions, paragraph, 85–86
travel, as idea source, 5–9, 34, 38,
50–51, 57, 92, 138
travel article, 11, 17–19, 98–99
idea sources for, 34, 57. *See also*
ideas, sources for
markets for, 18. *See also* markets,
sales
research for, 5–6
travel magazines, as market, 18
typewriter, as writing tool, 41, 44–45

U
universal wants, 21
unsolicited queries, 116
unsolicited submissions, 64, 115, 116,
118
U.S. Government Printing Office, 36

V
Venice Interactive Community (VIC),
37
verse lead, 75
vitamins, as subject, 22
voice recognition software, 42

W
Wall Street Journal, the, 130
Web sites, 4, 18
and online magazines, 130, 133
use of, for marketing, 129–130
use of photographs in, 97. *See also*
Internet
Web-TV (article), 83
"What Farmers Think of Family
Farms" (article), 99
White, E. B., 47

who, what, when, where, and why
(Five *W*s), 59–63
in lead paragraph, 73
Wilbur, L. P., 171, 176, 181, 184
and anecdotes, 92
and article rejection, 126
and article rewrites, 139
and article titles, 69, 70
Coca-Cola article, 99–101
and commands, as idea source, 54
and general interest article, 14
and greeting card ideas, 141
and interviews, 16, 27, 104
and lead paragraphs, 73–74
and paragraph transitions, 85
reincarnation article, 52, 166–168
road rage article, 12
self-help article, 24
and sources for ideas, 50
and travel writing, 5–6, 7, 30–31
and use of statistics, 95
and "who" question, in structure, 60
writing schedule, 41
Will to Believe, The, 23
Wired (online magazine), 133
Woodward, Helen, 140
word count, and parsing method,
65–66
word processing software, 42, 45
working hours. *See* schedule, writing
work methods, 144–146, 150, 151
of famous writers, 47

and idea folder, 33–34
and parsing method, 65–66
and writing schedule, 3–4, 45–46,
65–66, 143, 147, 151
Write Markets Report, 118
writers, traits of, 149
writer's block, 79, 148
Writer's Digest, 141, 146
Writer's Guidelines Database, 113
Writer's Market, 44, 64, 112, 141, 142,
146
writing, article
advantages of, 2–4, 9, 143, 146
as lifestyle choice, 2–4, 9, 143,
146, 151
multiple articles in progress, 88, 148
office space for, 43, 79, 144, 149
for specific markets, 112, 126
as storytelling, 6–9, 90
tips for, 33–34, 48, 89, 113–114, 131
tools for, 41–45
work methods for. *See* work methods
writing journal, 39, 53, 54
Writing the Creative Article, 13

Y
Yahoo! (search engine), 107
Yudkin, Marcia, 39

Z
'zines. *See* online magazines
zodiac, as idea source, 55

About the Authors

L. PERRY WILBUR is the author of more than five thousand published articles and twenty books including *The Fast Track to Success*, *Dream Big*, *Getting Up When You're Down*, *Money in Your Mailbox*, and *How to Write Books That Sell* (with Jon Samsel). He is a prolific speaker who has spoken to business, civic, and patriotic organizations; school and college groups; women's clubs; churches; and numerous other associations. He lives in Jacksonville, Florida.

JON SAMSEL is a technology consultant, author, and writing instructor. He is the coauthor of *Writing For Interactive Media*, *How To Write Books That Sell*, and *Dead Ahead: The Web Dilemma and the New Rules of Business*. He also wrote and produced *The Killer Content Workbook*, an interactive developer guide for Apple Computer.

Samsel has taught writing at UC Irvine Extension and at the famed Writer's Program at UCLA Extension.

Books from Allworth Press

How to Write Books That Sell, Second Edition by L. Perry Wilbur and Jon Samsel (hardcover, 6 × 9, 224 pages, $19.95)

Writing for Interactive Media: The Complete Guide by Jon Samsel and Darryl Wimberley (hardcover, 6 × 9, 320 pages, $19.95)

The Writer's and Photographer's Guide to Global Markets by Michael Sedge (hardcover, 6 × 9, 288 pages, $19.95)

The Writer's Legal Guide, Second Edition by Tad Crawford and Tony Lyons (hardcover, 6 × 9, 320 pages, $19.95)

Business and Legal Forms for Authors and Self-Publishers, Revised Edition by Tad Crawford (softcover, 8½ × 11, 192 pages, $19.95)

This Business of Publishing: An Insider's View of Current Trends and Tactics by Richard Curtis (softcover, 6 × 9, 224 pages, $18.95)

The Writer's Resource Handbook by Daniel Grant (softcover, 6 × 9, 272 pages, $19.95)

Mastering the Business of Writing: A Leading Literary Agent Reveals the Secrets of Success by Richard Curtis (softcover, 6 × 9, 272 pages, $18.95)

The Internet Research Guide, Revised Edition by Timothy K. Maloy (softcover, 6 × 9, 208 pages, $18.95)

The Writer's Internet Handbook by Timothy K. Maloy (softcover, 6 × 9, 192 pages, $18.95)

The Writer's Guide to Corporate Communications by Mary Moreno (softcover, 6 × 9, 192 pages, $18.95)

Please write to request our free catalog. To order by credit card, call 1-800-491-2808 or send a check or money order to Allworth Press, 10 East 23rd Street, Suite 210, New York, NY 10010. Include $5 for shipping and handling for the first book ordered and $1 for each additional book. Ten dollars plus $1 for each additional book if ordering from Canada. New York State residents must add sales tax.

To see our complete catalog on the World Wide Web, or to order online, you can find us at *www.allworth.com*.